Bible Coach
Devotionals
90 Days

INSPIRATION THAT
ILLUSTRATES THE SOUL

DUNAMIS DUPLESSIS

ISBN: 978-1-6847-0357-9 (sc)
ISBN: 978-1-6847-0758-4 (hc)
ISBN: 978-1-6847-0356-2 (e)

Lulu Publishing Services rev. date: 05/09/2019

CONTENTS

DEDICATION

I want to thank every Christian author that has inspired me to write "Bible Coach Devotionals." The list of the authors are. Joyce Meyers, Bishop TD Jakes, Os Hillman, Sarah Young, Max Lucado, John Maxwell, Rick Warren, Les Brown, and Charles Stanley. Now I appreciate the long hours of commitment and consistency it takes to write life-changing inspiration that stick to the heart and soul of the reader.

To my brother Dan Duplessis for modeling the excellence of a great leader not only as a father but also as a newly promoted major in the U.S Army. To my father Bishop Donald L Duplessis Sr for enduring 20 years of military service as naval officer combined with 30 years in full-time ministry overseas in Japan. To my mother Pastor Evelyn Duplessis for inspiring and representing unique approaches in how to study, pray, engage in the word of God on a daily basis. I honor the Christ that stands tall in you're life. You have shown me everything I know today relating to Gods word in action. The long nights of prayer together, the strict accountability you displayed when I missed the mark falling short in my faith in God. I love you with all my heart. To my youngest brother Josh for giving me a chance to prayer over every situation you faced from boy to man. You are brilliantly smart with an IQ that still blows my mind to this day. To all my friends behind the scenes, you know who you are. To pastor, Kevin Willams thank you for you're mentorship, passion, grace, and stamp of approval for this project. I would have never thought a man of God living in the UK would be such an inspiration to me. I want to honor your family thank for your heart and passion for God.

INTRODUCTION

My life started in Honolulu Hawaii July 23, 1980. Nurtured in a Godly up-bringing and home bridged my zeal for God in a powerful way. Options to hang out with friends after going to church was always limited due to strict moral up brings. I lived a life of constant travel when my father completed staff college for naval officer training. The first duty station was Hawaii. After four years my family moved to Japan for new orders. At the age of four, my parents enrolled me in a Japanese American private school. I mastered the curriculum of learning how to be fluent and efficient in Japanese. After graduating from high school overseas in 1998, I moved to San Antonio, Texas. A few months later I was fortunate to sign documents to be enlisted in the U.S Army as an infantryman in the 82nd Airborne Division in Fort Bragg, NC. Years later I returned to Japan in 2009 to be a full-time English instructor in Yokohama. On March 11th, 2011 I witnessed and survived one of the most catastrophic earthquakes in Japanese history. The 9.1 aftershocks deepen my love for God knowing that God spared my life for a higher calling. In 2014 I worked as a fisherman in Dutch Harbor, Alaska. I experienced living through a two day storm that almost took my life the second time. I knew there had to be more profound reasons for me living through two death experiences of testing. My life was never consistent with one job; I always moved from position to post. I dated in and out of the church but never settled down.

My intentions were great but my spiritual foundation living alone and independent was never really concrete and secure. Went from church to church, went through stages of depression, my diet changed due to self-awareness of repeated family history of diabetes and high blood pressure. Church friends felt like worldly friends and Sunday messages all appeared to be the same. My true calling was public speaking, motivational coaching and writing. I discovered that ministry was in my blood regardless if I believed or not. I was never pressured by my father to be involved in ministry. With both parents heavily involved in ministry I was never compelled into a position of a minister. I honestly thought I wasn't good enough to live in the same shoes as my father. After careful assessment and extended hours of collective thoughts and prayer, God gave me Bible Coach Devotionals. I'm grateful, honored, and blessed to have family and friends that support and believe this would happen from start to finish.

DAY 1

CREATION

In the beginning God created the heavens and the earth. Now the earth
was formless and empty, darkness was over the surface of the deep,
and the Spirit of God was hovering over the face of the waters.

GENESIS 1:1-2

Every mountain, tree, plant, insect, and mammal plays a crucial role in the cosmos of God's creative order. Scientists, scholars, and archeologists have conjured, debated, researched, and assessed views and opinions as to the existence of God and His role as Creator. Genesis is known as the book of beginnings. Three important pointers highlight the power of God's Creation: Creation itself, sin, and the image of God. In Creation, we see the harmony of God to man, man to creature, and creature to nature.

Scripture Illustration

In the first three verses of Genesis, the Bible says that God created the heavens and the earth. The earth was waste and void, and darkness was upon the surface of the deep. God already had in mind the kind of creational canvas he desired. He began plugging, connecting, arranging, lifting, smoothing and aligning His ideas and revealing the vision for how He wanted the world created. We should never question the power of God. After all, He is the One who spoke the beginning into reality. He extended the east, west, north, and south on purpose. He made sure that if any other gods claimed to be greater, that god would have to surpass Creation. Everything God created included precise detail, structure, and order with no room for failure. (Read: Genesis 1)

Devotional Take Away

It's nothing like taking a moment to look at Gods creation in awe. I can honestly say that I am blessed to have the things I have. Essential amenities, gas in my car, food on the table, breath in my lungs, family and friends that care about my well begin, a shelter for rest and most importantly life, health, and strength. Gods plan and agenda always supersede the well thought out plans we might have had for the future. Your blessed even when you don't feel blessed, your still covered even when you don't feel covered. God is in a category of His own; His creative canvas needs no introduction.

DAY 2

IN SEVEN DAYS

By the seventh day God had finished the work he had been doing; so on the seventh day he rested from all his work. Then God blessed the seventh day and made it holy, because on it he rested from all the work of creating that he had done.

GENESIS 2:2-3

God's creative power exudes a unique brilliance of divine greatness. Over the years, I've experienced real experiences out at sea as a fisherman. After traveling by sea for days on end, waiting to catch fish, I have a deeper appreciation for God's creation. There is no question that God exists. He gave life to man, created seed-bearing fruit, vegetation, plants, and trees. God created light in the vault of the sky, separating the day from the night. He created a greater light and a lesser light to distinguish the sequence of morning, afternoon, evening, and night.

Scripture Illustration

God gave to man seed-bearing plants and every fruit, bearing seed within seed for consumption and survival. God knew that everything He had created needed regular access to food. Every cycle of food gave birth to new creatures and livestock. God used rhythm and consistency to build a formation of sustenance within His creation. In our daily work-related progress, we see proof and evidence of God's existence. (Read: Genesis 2)

Devotional Take Away

Regardless if you're starting or well-seasoned in your relationship with God, it's vital that your love for God goes beyond religion and ritual. God can see way past the tenth step of the tenth year you're trying to plan for, He might even reveal bits and pieces of the plan in-between season. If God revealed the end to you, it would probably overwhelm you. My prayer is that you surround yourself with true believers who possess the purest form of respect and reverence for God. When you completely surrender to God, new elements of passion, purpose, and grace never ends.

DAY 3

ADAM & EVE

So the LORD God caused the man to fall into a deep sleep; and while
he was sleeping, he took one of the man's ribs and then closed up the
place with flesh. Then the LORD God made a woman from the rib
he had taken out of the man, and he brought her to the man.

GENESIS 2:21

In the setting of the garden of Eden, everything had structure, sequence, and order. The Bible indicates a specific detail that at times is overlooked by the church
at large. In the context of the story of Adam and Eve, Genesis 2:5 says that no
shrub had yet appeared on the earth and no plant had yet sprung up. A shrub
is a woody plant that is smaller than a tree, with stems rising from the ground.
God's attention to detail was specific even towards the new growth that came
from the earth. He didn't cause the clouds to bring rain to the soil to cause new
plants to grow before He had made Adam and Eve care for them.

Scripture Illustration

In Genesis 2:21, The lord assets Adam situations and noticed that he was
lonely and needed a helpmate. God cause Adam to fall into a deep sleep, and
while he was sleeping, he took out a rib from his flesh to create Eve. After the
removal of the rib, the bible says that God brought her to the man. The significance of this moment shows the authority and leadership of God working
through Adam as the actual covering of Eve and the Garden. (Read: Genesis 2)

Devotional Take Away

The issue confronting most couple stems from the root of intimacy before
marriage. Intimacy before marriage is entirely contrary to Gods plan. If intimacy
before marriage is your concern, Let your prayer be that you allow God to work in
your life concerning stages leading to marriage. God sees everything and knows
the hidden desires of the soul. The worst feeling in the world is repeated guilt
caused by acts of sexual sin. When the same sin was committed on Saturday,
church on Sunday morning feels uncomfortable knowing the weight of guilt from
the sinful acts of the previous night. I encourage you to protect your heart, your
feelings, and your body.

DAY 4

GARDEN TEMPTATIONS

*Now the serpent was more crafty than any of the wild animals
the Lord God had made. He said to the woman, 'Did God really
say, "You must not eat from any tree in the garden"?'*

GENESIS 3:1

Disobedience in the eyes of God holds various weights of accountability. In life, we tend to blame others for the mistakes we initially choose for ourselves. What makes the enemy so crafty that we don't see his game plan before it happens? The enemy studies environments just as much as we do. The fall of man and the repercussions that came with quick decisions led to distrust, dishonor and judgment. God knows you well enough to test your love for Him. The gut feeling of wisdom is subtle. The moment you go out with friends and you sense a fight about to break out is the gut feeling of Gods wisdom speaking through you. Eve could have avoided the temptation of the serpent, but she lacked the covering of Adam teaching her the signs and signals of temptation.

Scripture Illustration

The serpent was smart and crafty; he must have heard the instructions given to Adam and Eve. The serpent asked, "Did God say you must not eat from any tree in the garden?" Isn't it ironic how the Enemy rearranges questions to make God's Word look foolish? The Enemy must have nagged Eve continually to the point she began believing the lies of the Serpent's deception. (Read: Genesis 3)

Devotional Take Away

Let this story serve as a teaching tool on how to avoid being tempted by the things of this world. Friends, family, and co-workers may have opinions and viewpoints about specific issues, but we must never let circumstances, gossip, and lies get the best of us or dampen our belief in God. We can overcome temptation with the love of God and show others that there is more to life than the typical approach of the enemy. The more you yield to God, the more your actions line up with your purpose. God is not a patty-cake God that you play with when you need Him to show you a sign. God has to trust you to live out what His signs are implying. The signs He gives are visual props that confirm He is God, regardless of whether people believe the signs or not.

CAIN'S JEALOUSY

The Lord looked with favor on Abel and his offering, but on Cain and his offering he did not look with favor. So Cain was very angry, and his face was downcast.

GENESIS 4:4-5

We tend to hide our jealousy behind closed doors. I believe that everyone has had moments of jealousy in their life. Jealousy can show up when your best friend who is a co-worker gets the promotion before you do and still the manager overlooks you, even though you have more experience. What about the lady or man in your church who marries the person you thought you would marry? What about the kids that you always wanted to have after trying for more than two years and then your best friend has a baby in the first month of marriage.

Scripture Illustration

Cain offered fruit from the soil to God. Cains connection to God was broken and completely off. He lacked the maturity to know what God wanted versus what he wanted to sacrifice to God. Abel, on the other hand, brought the fatty portion of the firstborn of his flock as an offering to the Lord. The Lord blessed and gave favor to Abel but rejected the offering from Cain, not receiving his sacrifice (Genesis 4:5). Because of Cain's jealousy, he became angry and nurtured hatred in his heart. So Cain set up a secret plan to lure his brother into the field with him; then Cain attacked his brother and killed him. (Read: Genesis 4)

Devotional Take Away

In the past five years can you remember a hidden feeling of jealousy that wasn't offered up in prayer? Now is the time to ask God for total healing of any animosity toward family, co-workers, church members, and close friends. You can make it happen; you have what it takes to shut down the thoughts and desires of jealousy. Psalms 30:5 says, "For his anger lasts only a moment, but his favor lasts a lifetime; weeping may stay for the night, but rejoicing comes in the morning." Embrace joy in your life; live free and have the kind of peace that attracts others to live their lives in the victory.

DAY 6

ADAM'S FAMILY LINE

When Adam had lived 130 years, he had a son in his own likeness,
in his own image; and he named him Seth. After Seth was born,
Adam lived 800 years and had other sons and daughters. Altogether,
Adam lived a total of 930 years, and then he died.

GENESIS 5:3-5

There is no surprise that the lineage and family line of Adam populated the majority of the world. Scientists are still perplexed by the lifespan of the patriarchs, the fathers of the beginning stages of life. So much skepticism and so many biases exist. Debates concerning the lifespan of Adam and the early fathers who lived in the days right after Creation have raised questions for years. Since the average person today lives approximately 80 years, how can these lengthy lifespans be accurate, you may ask?

Scripture Illustration

Before Adam died at the age of 930, his family line extended almost 10 generations. After the birth of Seth, his sons and daughters populated regions and countries around the world. Seth became the father of Enosh. After the birth of Enosh, Seth lived to see 912 years. Enoch had lived 807 years becoming the father of Kenan. It's important to note that after the death of Adam, the fathers that lived over 800 years of age before Noah came on the scene were Seth, Enosh, Kenan, Mahalalel, Cainan, Jared, Enoch, Methuselah, and Lamech. (Read: Genesis 5)

Devotional Take Away

You may be reading this now asking, how do I put this into real practice? Whenever someone raises questions about the truth about long life spans, we can go to His word. God shows His deity and power throughout generational life spans. Remember, it is only God who determines how long we live. It is God who knows the end from the beginning; it is God who formed each strand of hair on our heads, He is the reason why we still have breath in our lungs with a steady heartbeat. Remember that the God we serve is mighty, powerful, omnipotent, loving and gracious to us even when people forget how great he is.

DAY 7

WICKED PEOPLE

*The LORD saw how great the wickedness of the human race had become
on the earth, and that every inclination of the thoughts of the human
heart was only evil all the time. The LORD regretted that he had made
human beings on the earth, and his heart was deeply troubled.*

GENESIS 6:5-6

God could have wiped out the world with a few devastating earthquakes, but he didn't. Unseen murders, manipulation, idolatry, and hostility were all a part of the sickness that had taken over the world. God was sick of the foolishness even to the point of deciding to wipe out as much as He could, cleaning out the filth that lingered in the trenches of a broken society. God was frustrated with the dishonesty of broken people.

Scripture Illustration

The Lord's anger grew to new levels of disappointed with the corruption that flourished over time. God was preparing for the very first recorded destruction in the Bible because of the wickedness of a broken nation. God came to the point of regretting that He had made man because He saw more evil than good. The Bible says God's heart was deeply troubled. He must have had flashbacks to when He was creating the world, thinking to Himself, I took My time making all of this for a people that have lost appreciation for what I have done. (Read: Genesis 6)

Devotional Take Away

In our world today, we have witnessed the changes in our nation: overwhelming terrorist threats from radical Islamic beliefs and gun laws that make licenses freely accessible to non- citizens. Since the world is far from coming to peace with one another, there is still much work to be done. We can see the improvements needed to change the perceptions, views, and decisions people are making because of what they are witnessing devastating environments. To avoid Gods anger and displeasure in our life and society, let's remember reject the thoughts of evil keeping a pure heart at all times.

Day 8

NOAH BUILDS

The Lord then said to Noah, "Go into the ark, you and your whole family,
because I have found you righteous in this generation. Take with you seven pairs
of every kind of clean animal, a male and its mate, and one pair of every kind
of unclean animal, a male and its mate, and also seven pairs of every kind of
bird, male and female, to keep their various kinds alive throughout the earth.

Genesis 7:1

In the midst of corruption, violence, and disorder, God was disappointed with the sinful lifestyle of people on the earth. The descendants of Adam had to live in a world of disobedience, but God saw one man who was blameless in His sight. This blameless and righteous man was Noah. The Bible said he walked faithfully with God. That meant he heard the voice of God and discerned how to respond in obedience adequately.

Scripture Illustration

Noah had three sons: Ham, Shem, and Japheth. God gave a warning to Noah, informing him concerning what was about to happen. God pulled Noah to the side and said, "Listen, I'm putting an end to everything. I'm destroying the earth with a great flood, and every living thing." I can picture the shock and concern on Noah's face; he did not know that God would protect him, let alone his family and his way of life. (Read: Genesis 7)

Devotional Take Away

Are we shaken or disillusioned by small issues that rarely have anything to do with the big picture? Does God notice that we are still building and "fine-tuning the details of His blueprint for our life through our pain? Does the pain of building cripple the way you focus intensely on a task? Do you feel the weight of daily distractions from social media, friends, family, and obligations that slows the building process of a particular goal? It's always something or someone that gets in the way of the process. Real builders have a building mindset even when the toughest physically limitations get in the way. Use today's thoughts to build your dreams from the inside out.

DAY 9

THE GREAT FLOOD

For forty days the flood kept coming on the earth, and as the waters increased
they lifted the ark high above the earth. The waters rose and increased
greatly on the earth, and the ark floated on the surface of the water.

GENESIS 7:17-18

Imagine first hearing the raindrops, then the heavy force of the wind along with the beating rain against the ark. Imagine the ark moving and shaking from the force of the first level of flood waters streaming below the foundation of the ark. Imagine the screams of the people yelling for help, the beating of their fists against the ark in desperation, and the bodies and debris hitting up against the ark as it was lifted from the surface of the ground. For forty days and forty nights, the rain didn't stop. This had to be one of the most terrifying situations for Noah's family and for the animals.

Scripture Illustration

The Bible says Noah's wife, his sons, and their wives entered the ark. They had gathered every wild animal according to its match and kind. Pairs of every kind of winged bird, livestock, creature, and mammal boarded the ark. After God secured them in the ark, He gave the call for Noah to shut the door before the downpour of rain began. For forty days and forty nights, it rained and poured and continued to rain and pour. The flood waters rose to the heights, reaching past the treetops and peaks of every mountain. (Read: Genesis 7:8-11)

Devotional Take Way

From a spiritual standpoint, we have held things inside for years, yet we have never built a new ark to withstand the drama inside. We need a new Godly filter that will shut the door on the flood waters of our past. We can change are normal past perspective replacing it with a new vision of what God has planned for our life. God has a spoken word vision that can withstand any situation that is holding you back from being who God made you to be. Let this be the moment you let God know what scares you, hinders you, overshadows you, binds you, burdens you, or prevents you from facing the fears of your past. You can make it. You can endure the rain. It's time to float over the depths of your challenges and win with victory with confidence.

DAY 10

RAIN STOPS

*Now the springs of the deep and the floodgates of the heavens had
been closed, and the rain had stopped falling from the sky. The water
receded steadily from the earth. At the end of the hundred and fifty
days the water had gone down, and on the seventeenth day of the
seventh month the ark came to rest on the mountains of Ararat.*

GENESIS 8:2-4

Even after long flood periods of misunderstanding, hurt, and spiritual divorce, it takes new glass cloth to clear the smudges of unclear perspective. God knows the right time to bring you to dry land. Land symbolizes chance, opportunity, promotion, and open doors for security. Not believing in God's will for your life can keep you waiting with the dove in your hand. How many doves and Ravens have you held in your hand without sending them out to flight? So many people lack faith, even when they hold the physical tools of effort in their hands. It is not enough to possess the tools; you also need wisdom, consistency, grace, and God-given talent to survive and thrive in today's society.

Scripture Illustration

The total number of days of rain and flood came to 150. Most readers and storytellers speak of the forty days and forty nights of rain, but we must not forget that Noah's family endured more than forty days and nights of survival. I'm sure that after the hundredth day of living on the ark, rations of food, water, and daily living supplies began to decrease. Noah had no way to predict the outcome of the rain; he didn't know how long it would take to find land when the rain subsided. (Read: Genesis 8:5-8)

Devotional Take Away

Let God know how grateful you are today for those times when He helped you get through harsh life-threatening situations. God is all-knowing, kind, merciful, dedicated, and Lord over every area of your life. Trust Him to be your guide in every situation. Surrender every issue you have to God; He never intended for you to lack in confusion and discourse. Give every burden you have to God, let the toughest situations of your journey guide you into a new realm of real understanding.

DAY 11

COVENANT PROMISE

And God said, "This is the sign of the covenant I am making between me and you and every creature with you, a covenant for all generations to come. I have set my rainbow in the clouds, and it will be the sign of the covenant me and the earth.

GENESIS 9:12-13

We live in a world filled with broken promises. Businesses make promises to investors without knowing the real potential cause of outcomes. Covenant, according to Webster Theological Dictionary means "a formal agreement between two parties that establishes a relationship with obligations and mutual responsibilities." A promise is a commitment to an obligation to do, or NOT do, something. If I promise to do something I have the physical control to adjust to the measures based on my personal feelings. If God makes a covenant it's a permeant seal that never goes against His word. God illustrated a unique symbolization of His covenant using a rainbow as a reference to never destroy the world with this type of destruction again.

Scripture Illustration

God made a covenant seal saying that He would never destroy all life and the earth with a flood. The covenant was between God, Noah, and every living creature. The covenant applied significance with the power and covenant promise of a rainbow over the earth. Gods intentions showed proof of the sealed agreement we see today. (Read: Genesis 9:4-6)

Devotional Take Away

We should live our lives showing the same mercies that God displayed to Noah. We must show mercy to people who slander and talk behind our backs. We still must forgive them. God, with all of His grace, loves us more than we can imagine, even when we don't always do as He says. When we dedicate our time, talents, and gifts to the glory and honor of God, He sees that we lack nothing. Our service to Him is in the way we reflect the signs and wonders of His love in our life. God values our heart, desires, and actions over the visual symbols we use to display our love. What God sees makes such a huge difference in how we see love and forgiveness. His covenant promise never ends. His love extends from generation to generation.

DAY 12

NOAH'S SONS

The sons of Noah who came out of the ark were Shem, Ham and Japheth.
(Ham was the father of Canaan.) These were the three sons of Noah, and
from them came all the people who were scattered over the whole earth.

GENESIS 9:18-19

When a father raises a son in Godly leadership, the son learns to respect the authority of God through the father. When a father is addicted to drugs and alcohol, his actions automatically mislead the family on the wrong path. Going out on the weekends, partying, and following unhealthy lifestyles lead to a dead end road of immaturity when raising a family. Even if you are single and looking for the spouse, God has for you, this type of lifestyle delays and hinders the plans God has for your life.

Scripture Illustration

Noah was a farmer, a planter of the fields. He created a vineyard and drank from the fermented grapes harvested from his efforts. After drinking the wine from the vineyard, intoxication became downfall. He stumbled back into his tent, removed his clothes, and was found naked and drunk by his son Ham. Ham told his two brothers who were outside the tent to get their father some clothes. The embarrassment made the sons turn their heads to avoid looking at their father. (Read: Genesis 9)

Devotional Take Away

A spiritual detox is something that many churches and leaders rarely address. It's imperative and vital that a father shows the example of how a real man lives. People categorize fathers as baby daddies or my babies father. Anyone can lay down and have a baby; it takes a real man to run a house, cover the wife and children and provide without a handout from friends and family. When you build family principles on Gods word, you gain the order and direction of Gods counsel leading with wisdom, grace, and understanding. The instructions of a father that honors God sets the tone of how his family respects him even in the toughest times of uncertainty. We all make mistakes, no father is perfect, and no father never has all the right answers. Begin the positive example of how a father loves God, and his family makes a difference for his legacy and children.

DAY 13

DEATH OF NOAH

After the flood Noah lived 350 years. Noah lived a
total of 950 years, and then he died.

GENESIS 9:28-29

It's important to note that if you live your life in the will of God, He will bless the seed of your inheritance. The provisional expansion of Gods assignment makes room for itself. Your legacy means way more than a pay check of job security. What if something were to happen to you that led to your death, would you leave behind an inheritance for your family that holds the weight of multiple career paths? Will your legacy change the way others live? Will it impact the next generation?

Scripture Illustration

God granted grace, loyalty, and favor to Noah during his life. Noah faced turmoil, including adverse environments, sexual immorality, lustful desires, drunken behavior, and displeasing acts in the eyes of God. He accomplished a well-planned out goal of building an ark that withstood the storms and waves of dangerous seas. Noah lived longer than his forefathers, except Jared (962) and Methuselah (969). Noah was considered a part of the tenth generation of man. His name means relief and comfort. He brought some relief from the hard labor humanity had endured after God cursed Adam and Eve and expelled them from the garden. (Read: Genesis 9)

Devotional Take Away

Defining you're why is very important. What makes you want to live? Is Christ the center of your lifestyle? I don't care what statics say in broken environments. It's never too late to trust in God. God is still a forgiving and loving God. God knows your situation well, so well that He doesn't desire you to be discouraged. This is your season for the "rainbow promise" God has for you. He hasn't forgotten you, and He knows the higher purpose for your life. Live in joy and never let the Enemy steal that from you.

DAY 14

TOWER OF BABEL

*Then they said, "Come, let us build ourselves a city, with a tower that
reaches to the heavens, so that we may make a name for ourselves;
otherwise we will be scattered over the face of the whole earth."*

GENESIS 11:4

This story is so relatable to everyday life. Have you ever seen a group of people
caught up in self-made plans and agendas? Have witnessed marketers who come up
with ideas to dominate and control gullible investors utilizing power and money?
Governments, businesses, builders, and architects are not the angels we think they
are. If they exposed the hidden schemes and blueprints of how they acquired what
they have, it would shock you into real awareness. Your perspective would change how
you see life. Fame, power, and status can only reach a certain height before the rubble

Scripture Illustration

A new sense of intelligence came over the people of Shinar. They associated
intense work ethic to self-worth and power connected to worshiping a tower they
built for themselves. Shinar was the building site location chosen for the tower of
Babel. Babel means "a confused noise made by many voices." Shinar was in the
region of northern Babylonia. Ham, Shem, and Japheth were living in Armenia
when they decided to migrate to Shinar. The location of Shinar is where the
majority of the descendants of Noah increased the population of the world. The
people wanted to build not only a tower but also their city. The people were on
a building mission, complete with a structure of workers, tools, and equipment.
The people thought nothing would stop the process of their plans. Not satisfied
with worshipping idols, they wanted to become gods themselves. Their goal was
to build a tower so high that it would reach the heavens. (Read: Genesis 11)

Devotional Take Away

God wants us to distinguish the difference between glorifying self verses glorifying Him. The next time you talk to God or have a discussion with friends, talk about
the story of the tower of Babel and how it's similar to the world we live in today. You can
share thoughts with the family about how businesses build corporations for greed and
self-entitlement. It's ok to speak what's on our hearts after reading the word of God.

TIME TO LEAVE

The LORD had said to Abram, "Go from your country, your people and your father's household to the land I will show you. I will make you into a great nation, and I will bless you; I will make your name great, and you will be a blessing.

GENESIS 12:1:2

Access to everyday travel with Alamo/Hertz car rental premium packages didn't exist in the old testament. Abram didn't have frequent flyer points from United Airlines. His mileage points came from obeying Gods call on his life. He knew that if God told him to do it, He would bless it, and things would turn in his favor. I'm sure you felt moments of begin too comfortable in life. Some things take a real dose of courage, time and planning. I can honestly say that life never feels good taking on a risk with pain involved. Handling family responsibilities, work, school and obligations that require long hours of dedication come into play when knowing that it's time jump out on real faith.

Scripture Illustration

Most people who read this story miss the impact of the wear and tear Abram endured on his body. He traveled through deserts, woods, valleys, and mountains at the age of seventy-five. The first location where the Lord spoke and appeared to Abram while he was traveling was in Shechem. God said that Abram's offspring would take over the land and be blessed. Abram heard this promise and built an altar that symbolized the visitation of God's grace and presence. As he continued traveling, he stopped in a location called Bethel. He built an altar there and worshiped and praised God as a token of love and appreciation for God's hand on his life. (Read: Genesis 12)

Devotional Take Away

Suggested prayer: "God, it's a joy to know that you are God and God alone. Besides You, there is no other. You created man in Your image and took a section of man's rib to create woman. How great is your unmatched power God, when I hear Your voice, help me to know it's You speaking. "God, my desires for the world have changed. The viewpoints of my intentions have shifted into the new harmony of true purpose for my life."

DAY 16

SHE'S NOT MY WIFE

As he was about to enter Egypt, he said to his wife, Sarai, "I know what a beautiful woman you are. When the Egyptians see you, they will say, 'This is his wife.' Then they will kill me but will let you live. Say you are my sister, so that I will be treated well for your sake and my life will be spared because of you."

GENESIS 12:11-13

The severity of the famine was uncontrollable, overwhelming, and life-threatening. Abram and Sarai traveled to Egypt, seeking the best chance of survival possible. Abram devised a well-planned lie to manipulate Pharaoh and the Egyptians. He said to his wife Sarai, "I know you are a beautiful woman. If I tell them you are my wife, I'm dead, and they'll take you, but if I tell them you are my sister, we both have a chance of escaping death.

Scripture Illustration

After Abram and Sarai arrived in Egypt, the Egyptians and Pharaoh's officials saw Sarai was amazed by her beauty. Not knowing the truth about their marriage, they thought, This woman would be great for Pharaoh. The Bible says that Pharaoh treated Abram well for her sake. Based on the beauty and body of Sarai, Abram received cattle, sheep, donkeys, and camels, both male and female. He also acquired female and male servants. However, God stepped in, giving stress and anxiety to Pharaoh by placing a severe disease on Pharaoh and his entire household. (Read: Genesis 12)

Devotional Take Away

Our goal as human beings should be to have real, Christlike love for each other not compromising, denying or comparing our life to others. The world thinks like the world without second-guessing the outcome. What people view and perceive love to be might not always be a genuine love that goes beyond exterior feelings. The love that we search for should be love sent from God. His love covers every blemish, flaw, embarrassment, secret, and experience of your past. You're not the person you used to be. You were created to be the person God intended you to be. Walk in the counsel and direction of God and let Him handle the issues you may be going through at this very moment.

DAY 17

LAND AND HERDS

*Now Lot, who was moving about with Abram, also had flocks and
herds and tents. But the land could not support them while they stayed
together, for their possessions were so great that they were not able to stay
together. And quarreling arose between Adam's herders and Lot's.*

GENESIS 13:5-7

What do you when God blesses you so good it's hard to manage? Sometimes life
goes beyond the blessings. With all that God has given you what are you doing
with it? How are you managing the outcome of success? Obeying God can be
challenging at times. Second guessing, pondering and questioning God hinders
the possession of the promise.

Scripture Illustration

The herders of Abram and Lot began to argue in confusion over land and
space. They could no longer stay together because of the vast number of possessions. This account gives the first indication of Abram's and Lot's separation.
Abram stayed in the land of Canaan, while Lot stayed near the city of Sodom.
When God spoke to Abram, He told him to look around from the north, south,
east and west. God told Abram that He would give him many acres of the land
to own and manage for extended generations to come. (Read: Genesis 13)

Devotional Take Away

God's love has no boundaries or limits. God always finds a way to bless us
between the undeserved blessing. We shouldn't enter into disputes concerning
what we have and don't have. God has given us the means of wealth and security.
What He has spoken over the forefathers of the old testament still has power today. Without the sacrifice of seeking and pursuing, there can be no fulfillment of
the promise. If God said it, believe it, stick to it, and take action in it. It's not the
time to throw in the towel. You might be reading this now overwhelmed with a
lot on your plate. With every promotion, new role, new position takes a new skill
set to manage what's in your hand. My prayer is that God connects you with sincere people that support your intentions, goals, and desires God has for your life.

DAY 18

CHILDLESS

But Abram said, "Sovereign LORD, what can you give me since I remain childless and the one who will inherit my estate is Eliezer of Damascus?" And Abram said, "You have given me no children; so a servant in my household will be my heir.

GENESIS 15:2-3

Newlyweds, single women, and engaged couples tend to admire families with children. On the way to church, you might have witnessed a family with a newly born baby wishing that was you. You might have recently gone out to eat hearing a baby crying in her mother's arms wishing that was you holding a baby in your arms. The joy of motherhood goes beyond the aches and pains of childbirth. With every labor pain, contraction and morning sickness comes a true peace knowing that Gods timing is the best timing.

Scripture Illustration

Abram's life contained a vast number of possessions and blessings. He wanted an heir to pass on his name with the inheritance God promised him to cherish. Abram wanted his seed to inherit the blessings that took a lifetime to obtain. With hard work came the blessings of stabilized land, hired workers, and livestock. God told Abram to walk outside, look up into the sky, and count the stars he saw. As Abram was counting the stars, God stopped him, saying, "You don't have to count any further." The infinite number of stars symbolized the results of God's verbal promise of the seed of generations to come. (Read: Genesis 15)

Devotional Take Away

Stand strong through the punches and blows life may be swinging at you. Believe God and seek His plan for your life without wavering. Whenever God gives a promise, it might not be in clear perspective right away; patience in waiting is the essence of the promise. Married couples who are reading this now desiring to have their first child, God has not forgotten you. Continue to trust God in faith, obedience, honesty, and loyalty to His Word. It may seem like your effort isn't going anywhere, but in due season you receive your reward if you faint not.

DAY 19

TAKE HAGAR

Now Sarai, Abram's wife, had borne him no children. But she had an Egyptian slave named Hagar, so she said to Abram, "The LORD has kept me from having children. Go, sleep with my slave; perhaps I can build a family through her."

GENESIS 16:1-2

The story of Hagar is awkward, uncomfortable and strange. Today people understand this to be similar to the process of a surrogate mother. Most surrogate mothers follow strict guideline in carrying out a nine-month process through payment and contract. The flip side to Hagar version of the contract was to sleep with Abram, Sarai's husband to carry out the generational seed of wealth and abundance.

Scripture Illustration

Sarai was already frustrated with not begin able to bare a child. She approaches her husband as says "Go and sleep with my slave Hagar; this is the best way for us to build a family. Abram agrees to what Sarai wanted: sleeping with Hagar. The Bible says that Sarai gave Hagar to her husband to be his wife. The first problem was that Sarai doubted the power of God. As a result, she provoked Abram to a rushed conception process because of her pain. The second issue was choosing to create an atmosphere of premature adultery. (Read: Genesis 16)

Devotional Take Away

Have you ever been the victim of adultery or even fornication if your single? Many people in life are ashamed of exposing hidden hurtful sexual habits. The aftereffects of sleeping with someone who is not your spouse or to whom you are not married brings heavy penalties. Broke marriages stay broken behind closed doors because of hidden guilty of shame. Confession is painful, after the sexting, the lusting, the secret visits, and so on. Submit your desires to God and let Him handle your deepest insecurities. Honestly take the time to ask God to show you His will concerning your desires before rushing into decisions. The hard part is waiting, in the act of waiting the healing process that God releases will forgive and comfort your soul.

DAY 20

NEW NAME, NEW COVENANT

"As for me, this is my covenant with you: You will be the father of many nations. No longer will you be called Abram; your name will be Abraham, for I have made you a father of many nations."

GENESIS 17:4-5

Think about the world we live in now. What if God gave the same instructions to your family today? Imagine how they would respond? Some church members and friends would question the covenant and the intent of the circumcision. Why? Because true obedience to God's command never feels comfortable. It takes courage, pain, struggle and emotional conviction to deal with God instructions.

Scripture Illustration

Every male among them had to be circumcised, including himself. God said that every male that reached eight days old had to be circumcised. Every man who was in the household of the covenant, along with foreigners who purchased workers with money, had to be circumcised. God said that any man who didn't undergo circumcision had to be cut off from his people. (Read: Genesis 17)

Devotional Take Away

Many people might begin new journeys in church, marriage, and business. The reality is the process of figured out how to maintain what happens in the middle of the course is difficult. It's one thing to gain possessions, but it's another thing to have a team of people around you that support the vision God gave you. I encourage you to walk and live in the peace of Gods promise and not live in generic promises that lack sustainable value. People break promises and run, but God keeps his promises choosing you as his one. God knows when it's time for you to move out and do something about your situation. The problem with most people desiring to move out on faith is the simple fact of being shaken up while your moving. Don't be afraid to endure the shaking process of your fear. The colder it gets, the hotter you get, when it gets lonely, trust God to be your comforter. He said He will never leave you nor forsake you. Hold on to the promises of knowing that difficulty is a good thing.

DAY 21

SARAH DOUBTS GOD

"Where is your wife Sarah?" they asked him. "There, in the tent,"
he said. Then one of them said, "I will surely return to you about
this time next year, and Sarah your wife will have a son."

GENESIS 18:9-10

This story is a prime example of unreasonable expectations. Have you ever been in a situation where the instructions and assignment from the Lord seemed so out of reach that it felt like a joke? No, Lord. You can't be serious. I'm not ready. I have no money, my job applications are still sitting in the human resource room, and my medical bills are through the roof. God, how can this be happening? The raw feelings we face hurt the most knowing that things are still in the same condition.

Scripture Illustration

Abraham was sitting near the trees of Mamre relaxing when the Lord came to visit him. The Bible says that three men visited him, so at this point, Abraham wanted to do everything he could to serve them. He brought them roasted meat to eat and water to wash their feet; he offered shade to protect them from the scorching heat. Then all of a sudden the angel says to Abraham this time next year his wife Sarai will give birth to a son. Sarah just happened to hear what was going on outside the tent and began to laugh. She realized that her body was way too old to conceive a child. Abraham knew that both of them were too old to expect to produce a child, let alone Sarai enduring the intensity of childbirth. (Read: Genesis 18)

Devotional Take Away

Sometimes God puts us in the toughest situations on purpose for His glory and power to be manifested years down the road. God wants to take you behind the walls of doubt, directing your confidence and faith to cross the bridge of real purpose and destiny. Some of you are married with a child or children, knowing that if it weren't for God's power, you would not have a family. God's reasons are greater than medical reasons. When God has a reason for his result, it will change the course of time.

DAY 22

PLEA FOR SODOM

Then the LORD said, "The outcry against Sodom and Gomorrah is so
great and their sin so grievous that I will go down and see if what they have
done is as bad as the outcry that has reached me. If not, I will know."

GENESIS 18:20-21

How can wicked people expect to live in the condition of evil and sin without God's holding them accountable for it? The world we live in today has just as much evil as Sodom and Gomorrah had back in Bible times. People who seem to get away with so much still have all the wealth in the world, with flashy cars, houses, clothes, businesses, butlers, cooks, and assistants. I still ask God how do people get away with murder and wrongdoing without something happening to them?

Scripture Illustration

The evil in Sodom and Gomorrah was so great that the Lord wanted to completely wipe out the fornication, lust, incest, drunkenness, greed, murder, robbery, and hatred from off the face off the earth. Abraham knew that God was displeased, but he kept asking, "Why can't you spare a few good people? Why do they have to die with the wicked?" The Lord answered, "if I find fifty I will." Abraham went from fifty to forty-five, forty, thirty, twenty, and ten. The reason he asked the Lord these questions was for the love of the righteous. Abraham kept hoping that God would change His mind. (Read: Genesis 18)

Devotional Take Away

Sometimes people who are living right, showing kindness, giving to the hungry, clothing the poor, and building positive families go through more hell than the ones causing the hell. God knows the exact time to hold evil people accountable. In their eyes, they get away with murder, lies, and mischief but in Gods eyes, punishment is around the corner. In the corner of repeated adultery, drunk nights that led to a DUI murders, in the corner of child molestation, rape, and manipulation. God still has it covered, stay strong and know that your prayers of hope and justice will be answered.

DAY 23

SODOM AND GOMORRAH

Before they had gone to bed, all the men from every part of the city of Sodom both young and old surrounded the house. They called to Lot, "Where are the men who came to you tonight? Bring them out to us so that we can have sex with them."

GENESIS 19:4-5

Views and opinions towards same-sex relationships have different connotation and intention. The correlation between Sodom and Gomorrah in comparison to the disappoint God saw in a corrupt city. Many church members in leadership roles struggle with past experiences of same-sex relationships. Choosing to sweep sin under the rug tends to end in unwanted diseases, mental break down, double-minded belief and rebellion to the protocol of Gods intent for creating man and woman.

Scripture Illustration

The men of the city yelled, "Where are the men that came into your house to stay the night? Bring them out so we can have sex with them." After Lot heard their words, he tried everything he could to block them from getting in the door. Lot pleaded, "This is wicked and evil. Please don't do this. I have two daughters who are virgins, and they have never been with a man. You can take them and do what you like, but don't take these men." (Read: Genesis 19)

Devotional Take Away

Sometimes we need to have angels in our house to protect us from thoughts of divorce, anger, adultery, gluttony, hostility, molestation, and anything else that would break up a peaceful home. We sometimes have to make tough sacrifices to protect our dignity and spirituality. Lot made a horrible choice to give up his daughters' virginity for the protection of the angels. That's the kind of sacrifice we would never want to feel forced to make. You might not face such an extreme choice, but the sacrifice was a factor here. If you need to cut some people out of your circle, then do it. Do whatever it takes, never compromise your love for God. The Enemy comes to steal, kill, and destroy, but Christ came that you may have life and have it more abundantly.

DAY 24

LOT'S DAUGHTERS

*The next day the older daughter said to the younger, "Last night I slept with
my father. Let's get him to drink wine again tonight, and you go in and
sleep with him so we can preserve our family line through our father."*

GENESIS 19:34

Many preachers, teachers, and life group leaders shy away from this topic because
it's a sensitive issue compared to what the church is accustomed to hearing. So
here is the breakdown of what happened. First, we are dealing with the irony of
manipulation. Lot's daughters used alcohol as a mild sleeping agent to slow down
the process of their father's mind. When the mind is unconscious, evil has an
open door. After the door is open, the mind becomes numb, not recognizing the
difference between right and wrong. Deceptive measures of incest took place in
secret in a dark cave of manipulation. When the mind is shut down, it becomes
gullible and vulnerable to the lure of sin.

Scripture Illustration

After Lot was drunk with wine, the older daughter went in to have sex with
her father. The Bible says that Lot couldn't tell when his daughters laid down or
when they got up. The older daughter then told the younger sister to do the same
thing the next night. The two daughters thought their strategy would benefit the
legacy of the family name. They both knew in advance that they wanted children
and wanted to have their name carried on to the next generation. Lastly, they
were indirectly damaging the covenant seed of their forefathers. So now we have
two different tribes from the same bloodline with generations of children not
knowing their true origin. (Read: Genesis 19)

Devotional Take Away

The longer you live in sin, the harder your heart becomes, and the harder it
is to feel remorse. What I like about the stories and events included in the Bible
is that there is something for everybody. You rarely find a topic that someone
doesn't relate with. Let this story be an eye-opener concerning the events that
take place in a world we live in today.

DAY 25

ABIMELECH DREAM

But God came to Abimelech in a dream one night and said to him, "You are as good as dead because of the woman you have taken; she is a married woman."

GENESIS 20:3

How many times has God warned you or a friend in a dream? I'm referring to any dream that puts you on alert about innocently doing something wrong? In life, having a warning sign from God can come in different forms. Through dreams, signs, and wonders, God can reveal messages to make us aware. Some people refer to this as a gut feeling. This gut feeling can be a deeper consciousness, telling you to "pump your brakes" when a situation doesn't feel right.

Scripture Illustration

After this dream, the king did not go anywhere near Sarah. He questioned God in his dream, saying, "Lord, will you destroy a whole nation of innocent people? I did not sleep with her or even touch her. I was told Sarah was Abraham's sister."

God said, "I know that you haven't touched her, but I want you to return Sarah to her husband." The reason God wanted this to happen was for the simple fact that Abraham was a prophet. God gave specific instructions to the king, causing him to know that if he made any excuses about not returning Sarah to her husband, he and all his people would die. (Read: Genesis 20)

Devotional Take Away

God knows how to protect us from danger and harm in ways that we might not understand. He designs situations on purpose for us to check our lifestyle. He is the God of quickening and discernment. Without discernment, where would we be in life? We might be in jail, in a hospital, on the streets and homeless in a medical depression, or maybe even on spiritual death row. Asking God to heal your consciousness is the kind of prayer that can reach heaven. God wants us to stay connected with His grace and power. He needs something to work with. If we give Him our full attention, He will give us full discernment in return.

DAY 26

WHERE IS THE LAMB?

Isaac spoke up and said to his father Abraham, "Father?" "Yes, my son?" Abraham replied. "The fire and the wood are here," Isaac said, "but where is the lamb for the burnt offering?"

GENESIS 22:7

It's tough to comprehend this kind of faith in the world we live in today. Not only would a father spend time in jail for attempted murder, but he would also have to seek mental health counseling, along with a psychiatric evaluation. His wife and kids would be terrified, thinking dad was out of his mind. This unexplainable faith was used by God to awaken Abraham's heart and mind. Sometimes God uses strange plans to get our attention. If the task had been too easy, the weight of urgency would have been taken lightly, and the fear of the Lord would have been ignored. God needed the weight of uncertainty mixed with a life-and-death task to accomplish His work.

Scripture Illustration

Abraham kept his composure and spoke, "The Lord will provide the lamb." As they reached the location for the sacrifice, Abraham made an altar and placed the wood on top. He bound Isaac with rope, covering his eyes and placing him on the altar. Abraham lifted the knife to the heavens to sacrifice his son. While Abraham's potentially fatal blow was in midair, the angel of the LORD yelled Abraham's name. Abraham stopped and responded to the angel, saying, "Here I am. Don't lay a finger on your son; there is no need to sacrifice him. I was testing the obedience of your faith to see if you truly feared God." (Read: Genesis 22)

Devotional Take Away

God is not the author of confusion; He is the author of conclusion. The illustration of Abraham helps us to increase our faith in Jesus Christ. We might not always understand what God wants, but we can rest assured that there is a difference between standing still and moving forward. God is a God of forwarding movement, not a God of stagnant delusion. His plans and assignments might take years and years to finish, but in the end, God gets the glory and honor through the journey.

DAY 27

DEATH AND BURIAL OF SARAH

*Then Abraham rose from beside his dead wife and spoke to the
Hittites. He said, "I am a foreigner and stranger among you. Sell me
some property for a burial site here so I can bury my dead."*

GENESIS 23:3-4

Doesn't it feel good to know that God honors the dignity of ownership for the
right purpose for His glory? We can own material things that depreciate, but
owning the land used to bury a loved one has much more meaning than the
average purchase for personal gain. Honoring God for the right reasons goes
from generations to generation, seed to seed, harvest to harvest, land to land,
and family to family. We need to place essential value on things that genuinely
matter not on human-made secrets.

Scripture Illustration

Abraham was in search of a proper burial location. He was willing to pay
whatever the cost in finding the proper burial site for his wife. The Hittites
replied, "Abraham, you're a great man of God. The least we can do is give you
the choice of any tomb you desire." He asked them to intercede with Ephron to
make things happen. Abraham wanted to purchase the cave of Machpelah as a
proper burial site for his family. Ephron stood face to face with Abraham with
everyone watching and said, "I give you both the land and the cave. You do not
have to worry about paying me." Abraham stopped him, saying, "Please give me
a price so that I can have the contentment of knowing that I did the right thing
for my family." (Read: Genesis 23)

Devotional Take Away

We all know the feeling of losing someone. Regardless of age, race, or creed,
the loss hurts more than anything. Sometimes the role you play determines your
ownership of significant meaning. We all need the kind of ownership where we
pay the price despite the offer that doesn't cost anything. Always remember the
offer God wants. When desires are self-driven, the outcome surfaces into another
pay off without the wisdom of God behind the agenda.

DAY 28

SHE'S THE ONE

Before he had finished praying, Rebekah came out with her jar on her shoulder. She was the daughter of Bethuel son of Milkah, who was the wife of Abraham's brother Nahor. The woman was very beautiful, a virgin; no man had ever slept with her. She went down to the spring, filled her jar and came up again.

GENESIS 24:15-16

I believe God always finds a way to place people in settings flowing with blessings in clear view. You might sincerely do everything you know to do in honoring God, but it can't stop there. Put yourself in the environment of believers who think like you and cherish the same qualities of genuine Godly love for one another. Likeminded believers attract likeminded thinkers. Every detail that the senior servant prayed for Rebekah was answered and fulfilled. When God arranges the meeting of two people, he looks beyond the faults and taps into the heart of the matter.

Scripture Illustration

Isaac's wife had to come from the country where Abraham and his family had lived. Abraham wanted a wife for his son who came directly from God. He disapproved intermarriage with wives born in the same territory of the enemy. The senior servant said to Abraham, "What if the woman doesn't want to return with me to the land of Isaac? Should I take your son Isaac with me?" The Bible says that Rebekah was a lovely young lady, a virgin that had never slept with a man. (Read: Genesis 24)

Devotional Take Away

Even if you start out being friends with the significant other for a few seasons, make sure you seek God's counsel, mentorship, Pastoral leadership advice, and family friendship. As you are dating, it's essential to model cohesive mutual trust that bridges a healthy relationship on both sides of the family. Never rush into courtship, appreciate the longing of love that God draws in the canvas of authentic dating and marriage. When you include these basic principles and guidelines, the beauty of marriage blossoms into a covenant of purity established by God.

DAY 29

DEATH OF ABRAHAM

Abraham lived a hundred and seventy-five years. Then Abraham breathed his last and died at a good old age, an old man and full of years; and he was gathered to his people. His sons Isaac and Ishmael buried him in the cave of Machpelah near Mamre, in the field of Ephron son of Zohar the Hittite.

GENESIS 25:7-9

Passing the torch of legacy to the next generation is vital to consider especially towards how parents model the qualities of sound nurturing to their children. Leaving an inheritance for your children provokes a posture of trust in what God establishes starting in the womb. The effective discipline of teaching the next generation how to honor family legacy is paramount in this day and age. It's similar to having something to show for many years down the road.

Scripture Illustration

Abraham took action to build one of the greatest nations and generations the world has ever seen. The practices and principles you instill during the growth stages of your children impacts their lives considerably. Half of the time, kids are born into divided homes and upbringings. Fatherless homes produce fatherless fathers. Fatherless daughters produce broken mothers. Motherless sons produce acts of divorce built from broken promises. Generational influences are quintessential and should be recognized and understood in the plan of God. (Read: Genesis 25)

Devotional Take Away

Everyone should want to have some legacy to pass down to the next generation. Speak yourself back into a victory. Love your enemies even when it seems crazy. You never know when your enemies need help. They might come back asking for advice and prayer. You'll never know what they're going through until something devastating happens. Always be ready to share the love of Christ with others. My prayer is that you see the end from the beginning. When looking ahead, view the hurt that destroyed your forefathers. We should learn how to mend broken situations by living an obedient lifestyle for God. Let's refrain from making excuses about our past and embrace the harmony of genuine love for one another.

DAY 30

WOMB STRUGGLE

The babies jostled each other within her, and she said, "Why is this happening to me?" So she went to inquire of the LORD.

GENESIS 25:22

Seeking the Lord in prayer and evaluating the outcome before jumping to decisions is seen in the lives of friends, family, and our community. At times it naturally feels good to go with a gut feeling that initially makes sense. When we make decisions based on the flesh, we operate based on our outward desires. Leaping into marriage too soon, signing up for credit cards we can't afford, spending money for the wrong reasons, not holding the responsibility of weekly tasks can be a womb struggle in itself.

Scripture Illustration

Isaac spoke to the Lord on behalf of his wife, asking that she might have a child. The Lord answered his prayer and blessed them with twins. Choosing the things we want for temporary reasons might not always be the best decision in the long run. Sometimes, this becomes a struggle. Intimacy and love weren't necessarily the issue concerning Issac, but for some reason, Rebekah wasn't able to conceive. They desired a child who would pass on the name of the great leaders that had come before them, bringing glory and honor to God. (Read: Genesis 25)

Devotional Take Away

Weighing out decisions before making them final can make life so much easier when Gods wisdom is the core foundation of the leading. Seeking Godly counsel from trusted spiritual leaders builds bridges over the spaces of misunderstanding. Even if something feels like it might be a good idea still seek the Lord and ask if it's the best thing to do. God knows the exact time to step in when decisions and ideas feel ridged and misaligned from past experiences. The standards of moral motivation and confidence is still in you. You might have made repeated decisions that never ended well. You might have made two out of ten decisions that made you feel amazing. The decisions you make today can be a pivotal point of monumental change.

DAY 31

LIKE FATHER, LIKE SON

When the men of that place asked him about his wife, he said, "She is my sister," because he was afraid to say, "She is my wife." He thought, "The men of this place might kill me on account of Rebekah, because she is beautiful."

GENESIS 26:7

Often in life, the pressure of losing a loved one based on beauty and survival stems from lies that lead to fear. Situational scenarios present themselves in challenging ways to the point God starts flipping things back into perspective. At times, I believe fathers see how handling things in ways effects how sons and daughters handle things when no one is watching.

Scripture Illustration

In this story, we see the same scenario with Abraham and Sarah viewed in Isaac and Rebekah. The severity of the famine took a toll on Issac and Rebekah. God gave instructions for Issac to stay in Gerar and not move to Egypt. At the time king, Abimelech was king of the Philistines in Gerar. The men of the town saw Issac asking if Rebekah was his wife. Issac said that Rebekah was his sister, afraid the Philistines would kill him. Knowing that Rebekah was beautiful and was hard to pass by, he lied in deception to save his life. (Read: Genesis 26)

Devotional Take Away

Successful people go through the highs and lows of criticism. People in life love to see what they can get from you without giving anything in return. Always remember God is the source of your salvation and the road map to your destination. Begin apart of a spiritual inheritance results in planting generational seeds that flourish in any season. Bank accounts, businesses, and ownership could be passed down, but if God is not in the center of the business, the evidence will show. The favor of God is the result of wisdom. God is a God of supreme understanding. He causes kings, presidents, and prime ministers to travel the distance in respect of God's authority and power. Let the favor of the Lord be with you, even to the next generation. Trust in Him, wait for Him, and let God flex His muscles in your life so that your friends, family, and co-workers can know that there is a God who is true to His word.

DAY 32

THE STOLEN BLESSING

Jacob said to Rebekah his mother, "But my brother Esau is a hairy man while I have smooth skin. What if my father touches me? I would appear to be tricking him and would bring down a curse on myself rather than a blessing." His mother said to him, "My son, let the curse fall on me. Just do what I say; go and get them for me."

GENESIS 27:11-13

How many times have we felt this way around friends, family, and fellow employees? Someone sneaks behind closed doors to gain something they didn't deserve. In the case of Esau, it was personal. When you are dealing with family matters, the issue of hurt becomes more painful because it's right in the home. Think about the jealousy we sometimes see among family members who are fighting for attention, recognition, reward, and inheritance. When there is a family will, the father may leave his wealth to the firstborn. The contract makes it official. In Bible times, a blessing was considered a verbally binding contract.

Scripture Illustration

When Esau returned from hunting, he prepared a delicious meal for his father, Isaac. After Isaac told Esau what had already taken place, Esau's heart was aching with disbelief, knowing that lies had stolen the blessing. Jacob had stolen not only Esau's birthright, but also the blessing. The act of Jacob stealing the birthright caused division, brokenness, jealousy, and animosity in the family. Esau and Jacob wanted to kill each other. Jacob moved away and used the blessings of Esau for personal gain and deception. (Read: Genesis 27)

Devotional Take Away

When we go behind the backs of loved ones and family members to steal blessings in secret, God knows and sees our negative intentions. Feeding into the lure of quick wealth and gain leads to downfall. Everything could be going well in sin, and then a sudden tragedy happens. Eventually, the enemy finds a way to take back what we thought was ours. Obedience, and the way you execute the right approach can save you from the hurt and consequence of a stolen blessing.

DAY 33

BETHEL DREAM

He had a dream in which he saw a stairway resting on the earth, with its top reaching to heaven, and the angels of God were ascending and descending on it.

GENESIS 28:12

After leaving the town of Beersheba, Jacob began his journey to Haran. He grabbed a stone and laid his head down for rest. As Jacob fell asleep, he started to dream. In his dream, he saw a stairway that started from the earth and reaching the top of the heavens. He noticed that angels were walking up and down the stairway. At the top of the stairway, God was standing and looking down on the earth, declaring, "I am the Lord, the God of Abraham and Isaac. I will expand, increase, and restore your land one hundred fold blessing the seed of your descendants greatly. As far as the east is from the west and the north is from the south, so shall your blessing be. The blessings of your offspring will enrich the entire earth and reap the results of a future harvest."

Scripture Illustration

After waking from the dream, Jacob was in awe of God's revelation power. Jacob said, "This is the house of God and a gateway to heaven. I need to give this place a name." He used the stone he was sleeping on, placing it upright like a pillar and pouring oil on the stone. He called the location Bethel. Then Jacob made a promise to God that if food, clothes, and transportation were provided on his journey, he would know that the God of his fathers was the one and only God. He added, "Lord, of all that you give me, I will sow ten percent of my total earnings back to You." (Read: Genesis 28)

Devotional Take Away

We can learn two concepts from this story. The first is concerning dreams and visions. When God reveals a dream or a vision, it's essential for us to get an understanding of the dream. Interpretation of Godly dreams and visions can only come from God. Sometimes it takes a few dreams for us to realize that God is testing our response to His speaking. He may speak to us through a promotion, a proposal, graduation, a wedding, a reversed diagnosis, or maybe even through a real angel in human form.

DAY 34

WORKING FOR MARRIAGE

Jacob was in love with Rachel and said, "I'll work for you seven years in return for your younger daughter Rachel." Laban said, "It's better that I give her to you than to some other man. Stay here with me."

GENESIS 29:18-19

The customs for marriage in Bible times involved work and unpredictable twists of love. Most men these days are not accustomed to working without pay, even with the reward of marrying the wife of his dreams. Men these days pop the question after working one or two jobs to stabilize their life and produce an environment conducive to marriage.

Scripture Illustration

After the seven years of commitment was complete, Jacob told Laban, "I am ready to marry the woman of my dreams—Rachel." Laban prepared a great feast with family and friends. As the party continued, instead of bringing Rachel to Jacob, Laban brought his eldest daughter Leah, and Jacob slept with her. The next morning Jacob saw Leah sleeping next to him and was in shock. He immediately went to Laban, asking, "Why have you done this?" Laban answered, "It is our custom to marry the eldest daughter before the younger one. In order for you to have Rachel as well, you will have to work another seven years." So Jacob took Rachel as his wife and made love to her, showing preference towards her over Leah. Then Jacob kept his promise and worked another seven years. (Read: Genesis 29)

Devotional Take Away

As believers, we know that God ordained covenant marriage for one purpose to honor and please Him. What makes the Bible so intriguing is that the same mistakes we read about have been experienced by most of us, yet the local church never seems to address them. What better way to understand the stories and events of the Bible than through a devotional perspective. I pray that God rekindles His love in us so that our decisions concerning love are consistent with a lifestyle that pleases God.

JACOB & SONS

When Rachel saw that she was not bearing Jacob any children, she became jealous of her sister. So she said to Jacob, "Give me children, or I'll die!" Jacob became angry with her and said, "Am I in the place of God, who has kept you from having children?"

GENESIS 30:1-2

God knows that a single, unmarried woman might have an "I wish that were me" moment after witnessing a married couple with children. As believers, we should be specific in asking what to pray. Some people ask God for things they're not truly ready to handle. When marriage is unstable by secret text messages, lustful desires, wild parties, and promiscuous activity, things naturally can turn sour: sour in communication, sour in interest, sour in trust, sour in health, and sour in God's judgment of sin.

Scripture Illustration

Leah became pregnant, giving birth to Reuben, Simeon, Levi, and Judah. Rachel became jealous of Leah, knowing that the Lord was blessing Leah's womb over her own. She demanded that Jacob give her children or she would die. Jacob was disappointed, frustrated, and angry when he noticed Rachel's stubbornness. Rachel gave her servant Bilhah to be Jacob's wife. Jacob slept with her and gave her a son; they named him Dan. Bilhah had another son and named him Naphtali. (Read: Genesis 30)

Devotional Take Away

We were made to live in understanding, not in confusion. God gave us the joy of holy matrimony to protect marriage for His glory. All of our desires, dreams, and interests should be intentional without the Enemy throwing his typical stress games in our face. How many marriages have you witnessed on TV and social media knowing that the real pain is still going on behind close doors? Couples post what they want you to see, not what there really going through. People look down on the hard places of marriage for many reasons. It could be embarrassment, low-self esteem, manipulation and shame all mixed in one feeling. God has the power to bless and preserve your seed regardless if your married or single. Never waste your seed on dead soil. Place your seed on good ground so that the results speak in volumes, not in famines.

DAY 36

SPOTS & SPECKLES

Let me go through all your flocks today and remove from them every speckled or spotted sheep, every dark-colored lamb and every spotted or speckled goat. They will be my wages. And my honesty will testify for me in the future, whenever you check on the wages you have paid me. Any goat in my possession that is not speckled or spotted, or any lamb that is not dark-colored, will be considered stolen.

GENESIS 30:32-33

We might not understand the depths and changes in working for people who seem to have our dreams tied down. Jacob came to himself and realized that he could be well off by himself. Sometimes knowing when to move fuels a burning fire that goes beyond a wage that feels like a repeating pattern trapped in another person's destiny. If you are living in another person's vision and dream, your destiny will never come to fruition.

Scripture Illustration

Jacob went on his way, taking along his plan for the opportunity to gain wealth for his new life. Jacob cut branches from almond trees, exposing the inner white bark. Jacob's plan was strategic for a reason. Every time he would dip the sliced branches in water and place the strips in front of the drinking area, the flock would see the strips, and those that were in heat would begin mating. This plan would increase Jacob's wealth through more production and trade. (Read: Genesis 30)

Devotional Take Away

As believers, it's important to have independence, self-worth, management skills, building tools, property, and ownership. The beauty of life is appreciated in purpose-driven outcomes, not in uncertainty and shyness. Boldness is something you have to embrace when you want something done towards real professional change. We all want change, but not all of us have the will to change. Take the desires of your heart and mix it with the power of Gods will, and then you'll find change. The more you recognize the state you 're in, the more dignity and confidence you'll have down the roads of destiny and purpose.

DAY 37

LABAN'S ATTITUDE

Jacob heard that Laban's sons were saying, "Jacob has taken everything our father owned and has gained all this wealth from what belonged to our father." And Jacob noticed that Laban's attitude toward him was not what it had been.

GENESIS 31:1-2

You may know of a co-worker, friend, or family member that is jealous of the blessed life you have. A person with a jealous attitude knows various ways how to rub you the wrong way doing anything to get back at you. Feeding on what the Enemy is doing can cause violence, envy, and danger in the long run. You should never feed on things that are beneath you. Haters love to hate; gossipers reward themselves with gossip, non-believers find an excuse to bring up untrue things that others have said about your situation.

Scripture Illustration

Jacob began to notice a different side of Laban. What appeared to be sincerity wasn't. The Lord spoke to Jacob, giving him instructions to return to the land of his fathers. Jacob called Rachel and Leah from the fields, briefing them on the situation. He told them that he had heard that their father was jealous and angry about the wealth God gave him. He said, "I've worked hard for your father, but he has cheated me out of wages time and time again. I worked hard to gain the respect of your father, but my kindness has been mistreated for weakness. I must follow the call of God over the anger of man." (Read: Genesis 31)

Devotional Take Away

Destiny and destination go hand and hand. Mark the course God has for your life. The feeling of knowing God is with you is the confirmed assurance that your life is in His hands. Your aligned course might cause you to travel through seasons of delayed progress. Always remember that a blessing might be delayed but not denied. God will never leave you nor forsake you. He is not the God of broken promises; He is the God of covenant destination.

THE HUNT FOR JACOB

On the third day Laban was told that Jacob had fled. Taking his relatives with him, he pursued Jacob for seven days and caught up with him in the hill country of Gilead. Then God came to Laban the Aramean in a dream at night and said to him, "Be careful not to say anything to Jacob, either good or bad."

GENESIS 31:22-24

Whenever we have an issue with a friend or a relative, we should settle our disputes and differences with a Godly promise and agreement. Most of the time we became so angry and frustrated that we reject communication. We stop calling and instead play the "whatever" role. When things get out of hand, we should never run from issues but confront them with peace and wisdom. When God sees the sincerity of your heart, he will cause dreams, signs, and wonders to be revealed concerning your problem.

Scripture Illustration

The journey took seven days spent in hot pursuit of Jacob. When Laban finally caught up with Jacob in the country of Gilead, God appeared to Laban in a dream. God warned Laban not to lay a finger on Jacob. After Laban awoke from his dream, he approached Jacob and his wives who were camped out on a nearby hillside. Laban spoke to Jacob man to man, "Why have you taken my daughters without letting me say goodbye to them? Why did you run off without telling me? I was going to inflict harm on you, but the Lord, your God, came to me in a dream saying not to harm you." (Read: Genesis 31)

Devotional Take Away

Let this be a reminder to us all to learn from our workplace environments, households, and community sectors. When you let the sun go down on your anger, animosity, and resentment, subtle moments of heated emotion and hatred builds even while your sleeping. Going to bed without praying about the situation can lead to extended drama. The Enemy knows how to push the last button on your anger problem, but God knows your heart and your intentions. Take control and speak to the situation with wisdom and Godly understanding.

WRESTLING MATCH

So Jacob was left alone, and a man wrestled with him till daybreak.
When the man saw that he could not overpower him, he touched
the socket of Jacob's hip so that his hip was wrenched as he wrestled
with the man. Then the man said, "Let me go, for it is daybreak."
But Jacob replied, "I will not let you go unless you bless me."

GENESIS 32: 24-26

Many things were going on during this wrestling match. The length of the wrestling match was all night until sunrise. God was testing Jacob's psychical stamina with his spiritual awareness. God might be ready to reveal some new truths to you that will take you on a long journey of understanding. This journey could begin in the blink of an eye or through a stare of patience. The God we serve can visit us through encounters, revelations, lessons, brief words of wisdom, dreams, visions, and wonders. You never know what God will put in front of you.

Scripture Illustration

Jacob was traveling with his servants and wives across the Jabbok river at nightfall. After they crossed the stream, a man began to wrestle with Jacob until sunrise the next day. The man wasn't winning the match, so he touched Jacob's hip, causing it to move out of the socket. The man told Jacob to let him go, but Jacob would not. Jacob said, "I'm not letting you go until you bless me." (Read: Genesis 32)

Devotional Take Away

Seeing with spiritual eyes takes out the middle man and focuses us on the mission at hand. God can reveal name changes, assignments, moves, promotions, and ministry callings through just one angel. Never despise small beginnings; a small beginning could lead to a championship ring, graduation, a wedding, the birth of a child, and other real-life encounters. God wants to come into the deepest place of your heart and be Lord over your life, meaning God should have access to your heart and desires, regardless of what man says you are to do. We are the leaders of today and the go-getters of tomorrow. If God changes your name, something is about to happen.

DAY 40

LONGTIME NO SEE

He himself went on ahead and bowed down to the ground seven times as
he approached his brother. But Esau ran to meet Jacob and embraced him;
he threw his arms around his neck, and kissed him. And they wept.

GENESIS 33:3-4

How many times have you witnessed a situation where you thought forgiveness would never be possible? Fights with family, friends, and coworkers might have ended with slamming doors, throwing objects, cursing, and fists flying, eventually ending with wasted time and energy. Before your anger was a problem causing the same irritation of pain and guilt. Now the tables are turning, and now you think things through figuring out what went wrong.

Scripture Illustration

Jacob was listening to the conversations of his servants, who were spreading the news that Esau was coming with four hundred men to meet him. Jacob's first thoughts were of the adverse events earlier in their lives that had ended in anger and jealousy. Jacob remember the outcome of previous affairs knowing that he stole the blessing and birthright of his brother Esau. A settlement bringing peace and forgiveness between Jacob and Esau to took time to understand. (Read: Genesis 33)

Devotional Take Way

What good is old junk and garbage that has no value? When you throw away trash, you don't revert to it or wish you had it again three years later. That's what God is saying even now. God has placed certain people in your life to be angels in times of struggle, pain, and fear. It's time to hug and embrace the real heart of the matter. If we choose not to love our neighbor, how can we expect God to show His love toward us? God is the God of unconditional love, peace, and restoration. Let the love of God flow through you like a river that never runs dry.

JACOB'S DAUGHTER RAPED

One day Dinah, the daughter of Jacob and Leah, went to visit some of the Young women who lived in the city of Shechem. But when the local prince, Shechem son of Hamor the Hivite, saw Dinah, he seized her and raped her. But then he fell in love with her, and he tried to win her affection with tender words. Hamor said to his father, "Get me this young girl. I want to marry her."

G E N E S I S   3 4 : 1 - 4

What should a person do when a family member is raped? In today's reality, we know the possible repercussions when a crime of this degree happens. We know that serving a lengthy time in prison is the likely result of action taken after the sentence is given.

Scripture Illustration

In this story, the original plan appeared to be fine, but it ended in violence. Dinah had no idea what she would encounter after visiting some friends in the city of Shechem. She never thought her life could be damaged after only one visit. When Dinah made her visit, the ruler of that city, also named Shechem, set his sights on her. Prince Shechem governed and controlled all that went on in the city, so when he saw Dinah visiting his city, he captured her and then raped her. Forcing himself on her and defiling her body, Shechem perpetrated the rape, causing the gravest violation of her dignity. (Read: Genesis 34)

Devotional Take Away

The sensitivity of a woman begin raped can hurt a family to the core. Even though retaliation in revenge would be an instinct of justice, it only ends with more violence. Revenge is hard to live with. People sleep with it, eat with it, work with it, and communicate with it until they avenge the wrong that was committed. It's super vital that we seek God concerning the battles that we are facing. The battle is not ours; it is the Lord's. In the end, offering the unjust situation to God can save you from unwanted pain. God has the power to bring justice and conviction to evil people through the prayers you pray.

DAY 42

GIVE ME THE IDOLS

So they gave all the foreign gods they had and the rings in their ears, and Jacob buried them under the oak at Shechem. Then they set out, and the terror of God fell on the towns all around them so that no one pursued them.

GENESIS 35:4-5

The things we idolize these days come from temptations right in front of us: cell phones, clothes, shopping deals, nightlife, nakedness, drug addiction, sex, and fame are some of the many deliberate idols that we may face in the world in which we live. Many young girls pattern their lifestyle after personalities like the Kardashians. Some people want Sports Illustrated fame mixed with a look-at-me media fixation. You're not in the ultra-cool sector unless you have at least one million Twitter followers, and your Instagram page has to inspire an equal number of followers for you to be officially famous. The pressures people face because of media attention are endless.

Scripture Illustration

God instructed Jacob to build a new altar since the stench of wicked idolatry was running rampant through the fields and cities of broken people. Pagan Idols, earrings, statues, cultish garments, and ritual symbols were evident everywhere. Jacob instructed the people to give him all of their pagan Idols. After Jacob gathered the idols, he chose a tree in the city of Shechem and buried all of the idols beneath it. (Read: Genesis 35)

Devotional Take Way

God wants to filter out the idols that distract us from our focus and distort our perception. Reposition your spiritual lens to zoom in on the critical, meaningful issues of life. The material possession fades, but the heart of your intention remains. Whatever your heart conceives is a sign that greatness is hidden beneath the desires of your heart. We each need a personal altar on which to reverence God in the way he deserves. He is a holy and righteous God who never lacks perfection for a single moment. Take the time to ask God what idols you may be harboring in your heart. God can help you stay aligned with his Word when you dig deep into the realm of His true identity.

DAY 43

LABOR PAINS

*Then they moved on from Bethel. While they were still some distance from
Ephrath, Rachel began to give birth and had great difficulty. And as she
was having great difficulty in childbirth, the midwife said to her, "Don't
despair, for you have another son." As she breathed her last for she was dying
she named her son Ben-Oni. But his father named him Benjamin.*

GENESIS 35:16-18

An expectant mother wants only the best for her child as she proceeds through
the life-changing stages of pregnancy until the birth of her baby. When a mother
loses her life for her baby, a greater deeper meaning of love is appreciated. Many
consider this the ultimate act of unconditional love between a mother and her
unborn child. So many mothers never live long enough to witness the birth of
their child. Men cannot possibly understand the trauma of a mother's death
during labor and delivery.

Scripture Illustration

After Jacob and his family left the pillar of Bethel, experienced exhaustion,
humidity, and stress as they traveled. Rachel was pregnant, with labor pains,
frustrations, and long-winded stress. The battle between health risk and complications grew with the complications and dangers of pregnancy. Drained and
exhausted from pushing for the last time, she yelled, "Ben-Oni" before taking
her last breath. Jacob helplessly watched his wife pass away. As Jacob regained
his composure, he named his twelfth son Benjamin. Jacob built a burial site for
his wife Rachel in a tomb in Bethlehem. (Read: Genesis 35)

Devotional Take Away

Whatever God has for you it's really for you. God may put in situations of
sacrifice to test the character of your love for Him. It might go beyond childbirth.
It could be a sacrifice of leaving the birth of your business to pursue full-time
ministry. It could be a sacrifice of dying out to a toxic relationship in pursuit of
purity holiness to God. Whatever it may be, you can be assured that God knows
your heart and can feel the hurt and pain even when no one knows the real story
behind your adversity.

BIG DREAMS

Joseph had a dream, and when he told it to his brothers, they hated him all the more. He said to them, "Listen to this dream I had: We were binding sheaves of grain out in the field when suddenly my sheaf rose and stood upright, while your sheaves gathered around mine and bowed down to it."

GENESIS 37:5-7

How many times have your so-called friends and relatives misunderstood the dreams and revelations God has given you? When you show them your vision, they think you're out of your mind. When you reveal to them that this gift is for real, they shake their heads, not believing a word you say. Dreams have connectors, signs, outcomes, and journeys, but all dreams are not from God. Some dreams can come from the Enemy, revealing what could happen if you feed into the plans of this world.

Scripture Illustration

As the brothers' hatred continued, Joseph revealed a dream that made things even more stressful. Joseph told his brothers the dream: "We were out in the field, tying up bundles of grain. Suddenly my bundle stood up, and your bundles all gathered around and bowed low before mine!" His brothers hated him even the more after the telling of the dream. I'm sure they were thinking Joseph was already annoying enough and now this? (Read: Genesis 37)

Devotional Take Away

God sometimes reveals the strangest visions in the strangest dreams. Why can't God be simple and easy for us to understand? The depth of God's power exceeds the natural eye of consciousness. What appears to be odd and strange, God uses for clarity and change. Have discernment to know which dreams are from God versus which ones are from Satan. Your peers might make fun of you for your boldness in Christ but continue to dream and shoot for the stars. When God reveals the dream, run with the plan and cherish the stages and seasons it will take to complete the vision.

DAY 45

STRIPPED & SOLD

Judah said to his brothers, "What will we gain if we kill our brother and cover up his blood? Come, let's sell him to the Ishmaelites and not lay our hands on him; after all, he is our brother, our own flesh and blood." His brothers agreed.

GENESIS 37:26-27

God already knows if your family members are secretly jealous of you, stripping you emotionally and throwing you into a pit while you're waiting to be sold. Manipulation and crafty thinking can lead to jail time, death, and misery. If you only knew what type of pain you were bringing on yourself, you would reject the thoughts of revenge. Revenge is the root of the matter. The brothers had revenge and death in their eyes for Joseph.

Scripture Illustration

Joseph's brothers wanted him killed without taking the blame, so they thought of an idea to deceive their father. They captured Joseph and smeared blood on his coat to make it look like an animal had killed him. They assumed that the blood would be enough to convince Jacob that Joseph was dead. Reuben, the oldest brother, told the others to hold off on the killing. He said, "Let's strip him of his coat and throw him in that pit over there." (Read: Genesis 37)

Devotional Take Away

At times I have revealed my emotions and fears to so-called friends, thinking they had my back. What appeared to be a safe family environment was a cutthroat situation behind closed doors. God holds us accountable for both our actions and the lies we fixate on. Sometimes we know the lies are formulating, but we never pull the lie from the root. Never let evil settle too thick in the soils of your heart. Subtle evil grows into bold evil weeds that can choke the life out of a fresh harvest. I challenge you to examine which family environment gives off toxics vibes of negativity. Use the assessment for Gods glory to discern which family member is robbing you from living out the full potential God has for your life.

DAY 46

SLEEP WITH ME

Now Joseph was well-built and handsome, and after a while his master's
wife took notice of Joseph and said, "Come to bed with me!" But he refused.
"With me in charge," he told her, "my master does not concern himself with
anything in the household; everything he owns he has entrusted to my care."

GENESIS 39:6-8

Lust is a dangerous stronghold. If I counted on my fingers how many times I witnessed lust breaking up families and homes, it would take up much time. The lust of the eyes in a man or a woman can lead to serious adverse outcomes. Regardless if you're not caught the first or second time, the irony of guilt can destroy the heart and soul of the marriage. Most of the time, men pursue the desires of what they want. Half the time it's usually surface lust and not Godly affection.

Scripture Illustration

Potiphar gave Joseph authority to run the administrative side of his holdings, including the care of his livestock and goods. Joseph had the grace of God in his character with honesty, dignity, and respect for the man in charge. Potiphar's wife was watching Joseph closely, lusting after his body and his handsome features. She studied his every movement, flirted with him, and dreamed of being with him. The stronghold of lust overtook her to the point where she no longer desired the love of her husband. She said to Joseph, "Come sleep with me!" Joseph answered, "Look, my master trusts me with everything in his entire household. How would it look if I slept with you and turned against the honor and trust he has in me?" (Read: Genesis 39)

Devotionals Take Away

When you stand up for what is right the lie of the enemy only can last for so long. Lustful intentions of deceptive eyes can easily rip the coat of real purpose. The willingness you have to push away from the pulling arms of the enemy will save your marriage, finances, character, competence, and career. Obedience comes before the favor. The purpose and power to say no without verbally saying no means more than falling into the arms of temptation and lust.

DAY 47

CUPBEARER & BAKER

*"We both had dreams," they answered, "but there is no
one to interpret them." Then Joseph said to them, "Do not
interpretations belong to God? Tell me your dreams."*

GENESIS 40:8

In Christendom today the church struggles with the manifestation and interpretation of dreams. Nowadays if a church member has a dream and desires
the revelation of the dream, it might take time for the manifestation to be clear
in clarity. God gives confirmation, linking truth with truth. Your dreams have
answers, and God is the God of revelation and truth through the power of His
Word. The Bible never reveals the reason or reasons why the chief cupbearer and
chief baker were placed in prison. The baker was not careful with the security
of the food, not realizing that suspicious outsiders wanted to poison the king.
Both men had shared the responsibility of protecting the king in various settings,
and Pharaoh had been offended and angry to the point of throwing both of the
officials in prison.

Scripture Illustration

Joseph noticed that the two officials were discouraged and perplexed about
what they had seen in their dreams. Joseph asked, "What's the problem?" One
of them said, "We both had dreams, but we don't have anyone to interpret the
dreams for us." Joseph responded, "Wait. Interpreting dreams is God's business.
Go ahead and break down the dream for me." (Read: Genesis 40)

Devotional Take Away

If you take away one thing from this devotional, remember that interpreting
dreams is God's business. God teaches us something about the gift of interpretation through Joseph's life. God might test your gift to prove to you it's indeed
a gift. Outcomes and revelations are not always as apparent as picket fences on
the other side of the house. The weakness of the church is the lack of authentic
understand and evidence of revelation power. When God shows a sign through
a dream or a vision, He follows up with a witness that complements the power
of His word.

DAY 48

PHARAOH'S DREAMS

*In the morning his mind was troubled, so he sent for all the
magicians and wise men of Egypt. Pharaoh told them his
dreams, but no one could interpret them for him.*

GENESIS 41:8

Marathon runners tackle the pressures of long-winded pace strides for long distances. The longer the pace, the stronger the endurance level. God is longing to show you the pace level of your dreams. God is far from finishing the canvas of your dreams. He is slowly revealing signs of the dream in your life every day. God wants you to enjoy the carved-out course with dirty hands and sweaty palms before you reach the palace. If God gave you the palace too soon, you would treat it lightly as if it didn't cost anything.

Scripture Illustration

Pharaoh had two dreams that left him feeling unsettled. In the first dream, he was standing by the Nile River when seven fat cows came out of the river and started to graze on the land. A few seconds later, seven unhealthy, rough-looking cows came out of the river and ate the seven large, healthy cows. Pharaoh fell back asleep, dreaming a second time. This time he saw seven healthy heads of grain and then seven thin, scorched heads of grain. The scorched heads of grain choked and swallowed up the seven heads of healthy grain. He told both dreams to his officials, magicians, and wise men, but Pharaoh's staff still didn't understand the dream. (Read: Genesis 41)

Devotional Take Away

It's similar to hydrating spiritually when the heat waves of life hit the hardest. God wants to see you grab the bottle of water a few times. He wants to see you wake up every morning with the same passion you had the day before. It's time for your diet to change to fit the course of the challenge. He is building you from within, shaping you from without, and molding you into a finished work fit for the world to witness for His glory. God enables us carving out courses to help you appreciate the steps in between.

DAY 49

MAN IN CHARGE

Then Pharaoh said to Joseph, "Since God has made all this known to you, there is no one so discerning and wise as you. You shall be in charge of my palace, and all my people are to submit to your orders. Only with respect to the throne will I be greater than you."

GENESIS 41:39-40

We need Godly leadership and Godly government to propel us to the next level. Our conditions are indicators that God has a setup plan for us to see the bigger picture of God's greatness. His splendor, love, compassion, glory, and kindness are more than just a thought. It's a lifestyle that you live and walk out. Whatever spiritual famine you may be facing, God is about to reassign new promotions and positions because of your patience in serving Him in obedience. The hunger pain struggles are behind you. It's time to eat and dine at the king's table with kings that respect kings.

Scripture Illustration

Pharaoh witnessed a unique trait of God-given wisdom in Joseph. Pharaoh knew that his officials and wise men needed to be under Joseph's wisdom and direction to protect Egypt and its people. To be placed second in charge of Egypt was no easy task. Pharaoh clothed Joseph with new garments and placed a gold chain around his neck to signify the respect he deserved. Pharaoh also gave him the name Zaphenath-Paneah. At the age of thirty, Joseph was second in charge because of the power God had given him to reveal dreams. He also had two sons, Manasseh and Ephraim. God increased his household, giving him a wife he could trust and a leadership team loyal to the model and vision of what God desired for his life. (Read: Genesis 41)

Devotional Take Away

Let your desire for God be a secure warehouse of provision, covering and security. The more we let God protect us in the stillness of His power the more we will reap the benefits of an unexpected harvest of fulfillment. The course line blueprint of provision has a lot to do with how you manage what you have in your possession. God knows the exact depth of our assignment. Follow God's lead and never forget that He is the God of order, structure, and sustainment.

DAY 50

NOW THEY NEED ME

When Jacob learned that there was grain in Egypt, he said to his sons, "Why do you just keep looking at each other? He continued, "I have heard that there is grain in Egypt. Go down there and buy some for us, so that we may live and not die."

GENESIS 42:1-2

Have you noticed in the past how so-called friends and family hate you so much they desperately need you? When tragedy happens, and all hell breaks loose "Now they need you." Family members and co-workers may turn on you, but when they need their rent paid, they ask to borrow five hundred dollars. Your haters and enemies have hidden famines that are brought on them because of disobedience to God.

Scripture Illustration

Imagine the weight, fear, and damage Jacob and his sons were experiencing from a famine so severe that their resources and way of life were in jeopardy. Jacob's wisdom kicked in with a new strategy for obtaining food and provision. There had to be a way to make up for the loss of livestock and crops, but there seemed to be nowhere to turn. The only option was to travel to Egypt to replenish the household goods for emergency purposes. When the brothers arrived in Egypt, they approached Joseph in desperation. In their blindness and carelessness, the brothers didn't even recognize Joseph. Deep in Joseph's heart, he had the desire to put his brothers to the test since he knew who they were. He chose to treat them with respect and kindness. He questioned, "Where do you come from? You are spies. You guys are up to something." (Read: Genesis 42)

Devotional Take Away

God knows the end from the beginning and wants to hear your desires, but it may take more than three nights of prayer. It might take five to ten years to grasp the true power of prayer. Like Joseph, you will experience the "now they need me" moments in your life from the people you associate with. You might have to be the bigger man or woman and take the lead to forgive and forget. You can help them understand the hurt you felt in the past, along with showing the love of Christ in the present. Always be the example of forgiveness God desires, knowing in your heart that you are advancing in the kingdom of God.

DAY 51

BACK TO EYGPT

*But Judah said to him, "The man warned us solemnly, 'You will not
see my face again unless your brother is with you.' If you will send our
brother along with us, we will go down and buy food for you. But if
you will not send him, we will not go down, because the man said to
us, You will not see my face again unless your brother is with you."*

GENESIS 43:3-5

People are facing back-to-Egypt moments every day. They mismanage their finances,
projects, and business while taking God completely out of the picture. When God
sees the open honesty of your sacrifice, He will reveal nuggets that will help you get
to where you need to be in the long run. God is with you every step of the way. He is
your Protector, Guide, Comforter, Healer and Sustainer through the best and worst
times you may be facing. God has to push you through a challenge that's bigger than
you. Sometimes we measure the obstacles we face based on God begin angry with us.
Tough seasons are built to trigger the passion of power within our souls.

Scripture Illustration

Joseph's wisdom and discernment gave him the grace to put his brothers
to the test. He knew that if he gave instant access to his brothers, they would
have felt disconnected. He loved his brothers so much that he wanted them to
indirectly obey his command and authority because of what God had revealed to
Joseph when he was a boy. The brothers still had grain but noticed their limited
supply was running out. (Read: Genesis 43)

Devotional Take Away

You might need God to send a flashback in order to push you forward to the next
level of your dream. Dreams are not just dreams. Most of the time, dreams are visual
connectors, tools, and blueprints to what God is saying to us. Waiting on your dream
to be revealed can take time. While you're waiting, let God perfect a new perspective
as He protects your dream. When we ask God to perfect His gifts and calling in us,
He will show us the pathway to the end of what we have been searching for. The
end point might not always be what you want. Some people fight hard to get to a
end goal without taking time to understand what happens after the goal is reached.

MORE THAN TEARS

*Deeply moved at the sight of his brother, Joseph hurried out and looked for
a place to weep. He went into his private room and wept there. After he had
washed his face, he came out and, controlling himself, said, "Serve the food."*

GENESIS 43:30-31

God sometimes places the people that rejected you in the past at your feet in your
honor in the present. What didn't go well in high school and college is now the
position of a lifetime. In the present, you own the company, and the same bully
that hurt you in the past is now applying to be an employee under you. Joseph
felt the need to put his brothers to the test without revealing his identity. He was
battling to toes of emotions. The first emotion was the connection he felt with
his youngest brother Benjamin; the second emotion was the battle between tears
of joy versus the frustration of not begin ready to reveal his true identity to his
brothers.

Scripture Illustration

Joseph's brothers could not afford to ignore the instruction given by Joseph.
When the brothers arrived with Benjamin, Joseph began asking questions. In
between the love and concern for his brothers, he felt tears of joy and forgiveness
in his heart and hid in a back room. After protecting his authority and image,
he was able to pull himself together. He told his servants to serve the food, and
they served Joseph and the brothers separately for common reasons. (Read:
Genesis 43)

Devotional Take Away

What God is saying here is to forgive when the promotion happens. Forgive
when the financial settlement is complete. Never hold grudges for situations that
require forgiveness. These are situations we can relate to in our everyday life,
teaching us how to give second chances though we face a few tests in between.
You might not have the final answer to the hurt and pain just yet, but you can
still give God glory for what He had done in your life regardless of how bad it
felt when it first happened.

DAY 53

SILVER CUP TEST

Now Joseph gave these instructions to the steward of his house: "Fill the men's sacks with as much food as they can carry, and put each man's silver in the mouth of his sack. Then put my cup, the silver one, in the mouth of the youngest one's sack, along with the silver for his grain." And he did as Joseph said.

GENESIS 44:1-2

Have you ever been in a situation where you did everything right but still felt tested by God? You prayed, attended church, tithed, gave to the poor, helped out those in need, and still, God was testing you? It's straightforward to throw in the towel and tell God you're done with life. Sometimes God sets things up on purpose to evaluate the heart you have for Him. He knows the right amount of challenge necessary to grab your attention causing you to trust Him even the more. God could be chasing you down for a test already set up next year.

Scripture Illustration

Joseph wasn't impressed with the words and actions of his brothers. This time Joseph took the test further by using one of his favorite silver cups as a tool of testing. In Genesis 44:2, the instruction was given from Joseph to his servants to "Fill the men's sacks with as much food as they can carry, and put each man's silver in the mouth of his sack. Then put my cup, the silver one, in the mouth of the youngest one's sack, along with the silver for his grain." Joseph was so smooth that he didn't even let them get halfway into the trip before tracking them down. He told his servants, "Listen, when they get a good distance from the city, grab some horses and men, track them down, and accuse them of stealing my cup." (Read: Genesis 44)

Devotional Take Away

If you're facing a test now, it might be the exact time for God to show His power through your life. When everything is smooth sailing and secure in life, we tend to blow the appreciate process under the rug. Lazy snooze button behaviors place the mission and purpose of Gods call on your life on hold. I don't care how challenging life gets; you keep breaking barriers and walls until you break through with your head held high.

IDENTITY REVEALED

Then Joseph could no longer control himself before all his attendants,
and he cried out, "Have everyone leave my presence!" So there was no
one with Joseph when he made himself known to his brothers.

GENESIS 45:1

Some of you have loved ones that had dreams of playing professional football, basketball, or baseball. The door opened, and now they play professionally. Some family members would have never recognized you until the money was in the millions. They would have never called until they needed a favor. God is ready for you to show the real calling and true identity he planned from the moment you were born from your mother's womb.

Scripture Illustration

When Joseph was a nobody, they had laughed at him, hated him, despised him, and rejected him out of jealousy. Confronting his brothers face to face he said, "I'm Joseph, the brother you neglected and sold into slavery. Look, it's me. Don't be afraid." His brothers still didn't recognize him, so they felt uncomfortable at first. The more he spoke, the more they believed it was Joseph. Joseph reassured his brothers of his protection and safety. He explained to them that everything that had happened was all a part of God's plan. God's plan had led to the moment they were witnessing the fulfillment of the dreams Joseph had told them at a young age. (Read: Genesis 45)

Devotional Take Away

Your seasons of tears and struggle won't last forever. Your time is coming, and you are destined for greatness. What you thought was lost was just a temporary hold, giving the opportunity for God to flex his muscles on your behalf. Now you can grab everything you have and climb to greater heights and opportunities. Even when your gas tank was empty and showing the flashing orange light at the bottom of the red needle, God still made a way. He put just enough last-second gas to get you to the gas station in time to fill up the tank. God molds the humble and lifts the hearts of the brokenhearted

DAY 55

FAMILY REUNION

As soon as Joseph appeared before him, he threw his arms
around his father and wept for a long time.

GENESIS 46:28-29

The beauty of family members reuniting after years of not seeing each other is heartwarming and beautiful. The real joy of a son reuniting back with his father sometimes can't always be defined in words. If you're reading this now, knowing that your father was never there for you as a leader, protector, and guider this is for you. If your father neglected you, yelled at you, scolded you, blamed you, spoke down on you, and manipulated you, then I'm writing to the right person. Even for the sons who have fathers that are pastors, elders, bishops serving communities, nonprofits, and churches around the world this devotional is for you.

Scripture Illustration

Joseph's brothers rushed back from Egypt to the land of Canaan to tell their father the good news and status of Joseph. The brothers explain how Joseph is second in command over all of Egypt. The resources of food rations for the next seven years are in his authority. Jacob gathered all of his sons, daughters, grandchildren, livestock, and possessions in preparation to travel to Egypt. A total of seventy descendants included the sons and family of Joseph all arrived for further instruction from Joseph (Read: Genesis 46)

Devotional Take Away

Always remember God gives provisions, builds homes, assigns positions, delegates order, enforces justice, humbles the proud, gives food to the hungry, strengthens the weak, clothes the sick, and gives shelter to the homeless. His son Jesus Christ is the Savior of the world. He opens closed doors, breaks the chains of poverty, and gives confidence to those with low self- esteem. He gives assurance through His word and His promises. His word and instruction reflect the evidence of His power. When you take the time to meditate on God word, things begin to work in cohesive order naturally and unforced. Your winning season won't be won until God matches the hunger of your present to the fullness of your future.

DAY 56

LAST BREATH

When Jacob had finished giving instructions to his sons, he drew his feet
up into the bed, breathed his last and was gathered to his people. Joseph
threw himself on his father and wept over him and kissed him.

GENESIS 49:33

Experiencing the death of anyone we know brings discomfort. When a family member passes away, it's easy to question the reasons why. God uses experiences that include the pain of death to liberate, restore, and comfort the brokenhearted. In 2016 the death of Muhammad Ali, Prince, Fidel Castro, and Carrie Fisher impacted the world. Each of these individuals made a significant mark on the emotional lifestyle and thought processes of the people who mourn after they passed away.

Scripture Illustration

After completion of the mourning, Joseph asked permission from Pharaoh to bury his father in the land of Canaan. Joseph mentioned that he had sworn an oath to carry out his father's instructions in obedience to the covenant. Jacob was buried in a cave in the field of Machpelah in the same region as Mamre. When Joseph's brothers realized the impact of their father's death, they thought Joseph would be angry with them and hold a grudge because of the past. His brothers approached Joseph, saying, "Father gave these instructions to us to give to you. He said for you to forgive us for our wrongdoing." (Read: Genesis 49)

Devotional Take Away

God sometimes challenges our repentance level to see if our forgiveness level matches. Having a balanced life of forgiveness and good deeds is important. "Weeping may endure for a night, but joy comes in the morning" (Psalms 30:5). The joy God desires us to have is unspeakable and full of glory. We were meant to live and breathe like conquerors. We should design our thoughts to be in alignment with the power of God in us. Whatever it takes to be faithful in the small things, God places in us. Let's be faithful. Conditioning the mind to submit to the instructions of God can take our belief system to greater heights and depths.

DAY 57

NEW KING, NEW ISSUES

Come, we must deal shrewdly with them or they will become even more numerous and, if war breaks out, will join our enemies, fight against us and leave the country."

EXODUS 1:10

Many of us have witnessed past seasons of domination and control from a spouse, a boyfriend, a girlfriend, a college roommate, or co-worker. Allowing people or things to control the way you think is both spiritually unhealthy and hard to handle. I have seen a new boss take over a department with no respect for the hard-working employees who put in long hours of sincere work every day.

Scripture Illustration

The children of Israel experienced a mass population growth spurt that brought intimidation, fear, and confusion to the Egyptians. Pharaoh felt threatened because of the vast numbers of people that weren't Egyptians. The Hebrew women were strong women, bearing children quickly and with ease. Pharaoh knew the situation was urgent and decided to make the children of Israel slaves. He appointed slave masters over individual groups to make sure the work was completed in a timely matter. The mission of the slaves was to build Pithom and Rameses, cites for Pharaoh. The more the children of Israel worked, the more they increased in number in spite of the oppression. As the severity of slavery increased, the children of Israel began to doubt God. (Read: Exodus 1)

Devotional Take Away

God sees the hurt and anxiety; He understands the abandonment of rejection. At times, we enslave the thought process of our feelings numbing the calling of God on our lives. The waiting game of fear turns into a wasted game of mental slavery. The guilt of pain, negativity, and fear delays the outcome of dreams and fulfilled goals."For every new level, there is a new devil." The higher the promotion, the greater the responsibility. When standards are lowered, morality and confidence is thrown out the window. Lift your head, take charge of your dreams, and build wisdom around the trenches of your failures to prevent everyday stumbles and entrapments. Let's put control in the hands of God so that we can face the obstacles of life with purpose-driven destiny.

DAY 58

FLOATING ON GRACE

But when she could hide him no longer, she got a papyrus basket
for him and coated it with tar and pitch. Then she placed the child
in it and put it among the reeds along the bank of the Nile.

EXODUS 2:3

We have all experienced various levels of risk. Certain risks go beyond normal feelings, thoughts, and trials. Family issues, child abuse, phone threats, and delusional negative vibes are some common things people go through when taking risk with feelings and emotions. However, Imagine a mother having to give her baby son up for adoption to a foster home to prevent being killed by a murderer.

Scripture Illustration

Confused and uncertain, the mother of Moses made a basket durable enough to float on the Nile River. She trusted in the Lord with all her heart, knowing that her baby Moses might die or be saved! Her primary mission was to get her baby boy away from the death Pharaoh was demanding for every Hebrew newborn male. She layered a basket with tar and took other protective measures to see that her son would be safe as he floated in the basket on the Nile River. She even took her plans a step further by instructing her daughter Miriam to watch over the basket to make sure her brother was safe. (Read: Exodus 2)

Devotional Take Away

What happens when a person gives up on God too soon? Having faith in the wisdom of God will provoke you to track the process of your belief system. A friend who holds you accountable for what you believe is similar to the sister in the reeds tracking the progress of your dreams. The Enemy will attempt to kill you with challenges, tests, and obstacles, but somehow through the grace and power of God's mercy, you are protected from river predators, rapids, tides, and unexpected weather conditions. God is ready to save you as you float on the rivers of peace and provision. Your purpose must be protected. The Enemy tried to kill you many times before but it didn't work because of the hand of God on your life. Let's display the kind of action that extends beyond environmental distractions and focus on the of everyday struggles and fears.

DAY 59

HIDDEN IN THE SAND

He saw an Egyptian beating a Hebrew, one of his own people. Looking this way and that and seeing no one, he killed the Egyptian and hid him in the sand.

EXODUS 2:12

What happens when you lose ground as a result of a cover-up for something you have done out of protection of a family member? Guilt is like a cover-up buried under the sand. What if you were in a situation where one of your family members was threatened by someone from a different race and background? Let's say you were in a physical fight that led to killing the other person to save the life of your mother, father, brother, or another family member that you loved dearly. To get rid of the evidence, you hide the body in the woods underneath the dirt in the middle of nowhere. A few hours later you learn that someone saw the scuffle and, using a camera phone, recorded the video of the fight you were in. The word gets out on social media, and friends begin texting you messages saying the police are looking for you to place you in custody for murder.

Scripture Illustration

Moses was raised under Egyptian traditions and culture, but deep down inside he knew he was a Hebrew. Moses's style was different. He didn't feel the need to dress or talk like the people he was raised around. Something didn't feel right in his heart. Moses knew that his true identity was Hebrew. He needed to do something quickly to protect himself from the stress and anger in his heart that had been building up over time for his people. (Read: Exodus 2)

Devotional Take Away

We know that God holds us accountable for the actions we take, even when we are protecting someone else. We shouldn't run from sin without addressing God in repentance. Self-identity is essential so that life doesn't feel hopeless. The more hopeless we feel, the more time is wasted every day in trying to please others. At times God suffers feelings to surface to bring us closer to Him. Running from the issue doesn't fix the issue.

DAY 60

TAKE OFF YOUR SHOES

"Do not come any closer," God said. "Take off your sandals,
for the place where you are standing is holy ground."

EXODUS 3:5

At the age of nineteen, I joined the Army. A military recruiter connected my assignment to the 82nd Airborne Division at Fort Bragg, North Carolina. Still young at heart with a naive approach to life, I was taught to understand the proper protocol in approaching a high ranking officer. I had to be summoned or called by my platoon leader first. The platoon leader would then send me to the company commander, and the company commander would then send me to the battalion commander and the battalion commander to the general.

Scripture Illustration

The burning bush was God's way of getting Moses's attention. God called his name first to make sure Moses knew that there was a higher power speaking. He instructed Moses not to come any closer. God said, "Take off your sandals, for the place you are standing on is holy ground." God let Moses know that He was the God of his fathers, Abraham, Isaac, and Jacob. God also said that the cries of the slaves in Egypt had reached his attention. Moses would be the man for the mission of freeing the children of Israel out of the land of Egypt. (Read: Exodus 3)

Devotional Take Away

When you approach God, does it feel normal or rehearsed? Does it feel like you're putting on a show, or does it feel like you need to talk to Him? When you come to God, do you take off the weight and distractions of day-to-day issues? Does the prayer feel forced? Do you pause and wait to hear God before speaking? The protocol of how we communicate with God must have authenticity. Having a private closet or a room that gives you the freedom to cry out to God can make a significant change in your walk with God. God reveals Himself in ways that are not common to man's thinking. He can come in a storm, a wind, an earthquake, a fire, a child, an angel, or even a dove. Knowing how to discern if God is there takes a keen sense of understanding towards God's spirit and His Word.

DAY 61

SIGN PROOF

Moses answered, "What if they do not believe me or listen to me and say, 'The Lord did not appear to you'?" Then the Lord said to him, "What is that in your hand?" "A staff," he replied. The Lord said, "Throw it on the ground." Moses threw it on the ground and it became a snake, and he ran from it.

EXODUS 4:1-3

Have you ever said any of the following to yourself: What if I don't pass this final exam? What if I stutter in the middle of my speech assignment when I get up in front of classmates? What if the teacher finds way too many grammatical errors in my research report for history class? What if I don't find a wife or a husband by forty? Will, anybody, love me enough to marry me before I get too old to appreciate the wedding? The battles over preconceived defeat can cripple the process of God's assignment.

Scripture Illustration

After witnessing two signs, Moses still wasn't all that confident. God was coaching Moses and showing him proof of God's power and authority. Moses knew that his age and speech weren't the best at the time. Moses was forty when he killed the Egyptian slave master, but now he was eighty years old. Aaron was eighty-three but had a bit more drive and energy left to travel, speak, and assist Moses as an aid. When Moses said that his speech was horrible, God said, "What about your brother Aaron? Have him go with you on the journey back to Egypt." (Read: Exodus 4) Placed at

Devotional Take Away

When you have a partner and friend who trusts God and travels along the way with you, life doesn't feel as challenging. Having a buddy to encourage you, protect you, and laugh with you can help you and push you forward in greatness. God knows how to connect you with people in your church, life group, or team to propel you forward into your assignment. Just when you think you might not have the degree, qualifications, background, and job training you need, God will find a sign to give you to work with. God desires to give you what you need to work with. Not only will He give you the tools, but He will see that the sign accomplishes its goal.

DAY 62

BLOOD.....SWEAT & FEARS

"You are no longer to supply the people with straw for making bricks; let them go and gather their own straw. But require them to make the same number of bricks as before; don't reduce the quota. They are lazy; that is why they are crying out, 'Let us go and sacrifice to our God.

EXODUS 5:7-8

Days of blood, sweat, and fears build into rejection, drama, stress, and slave-like emotional environments. The embarrassment of receiving welfare checks, being homeless, settling for shelter homes, and losing time causes the fear of not having anything to show for even after the embarrassment. Working at a dead end job, knowing it's the only job available, can drive the mind into regular patterns of confusion. What do you do when you get everything right and still feel overworked? What do you do when gas in the car feels wasted towards a paycheck that barely pays?

Scripture Illustration

As we look into the eyes of the Israelites, we see the struggles of insecurity and low self-esteem mixed with blood, sweat, and fears. Moses and Aaron were sent by God on a specific mission to free their people from slavery. Whatever it took to do so, they would do it. When Moses and Aaron approached Pharaoh with instructions from God to give the people the freedom to worship God in the wilderness, Pharaoh would not have it. He was running a business with economic power behind every brick and tomb in Egypt. His power came from the things he built. The more massive the pyramid, the bigger the ego. The more he gathered slaves to work for him, the more control Pharaoh had over Egypt. (Read: Exodus 5)

Devotional Take Away

When you think life feels completely numb as a result of all the no's you have been receiving, God finds a way to reveal the hidden yes connected to your victory. God is strategic with well-thought-out plans that extend beyond the present. The simple fact that God has the power to keep our hearts beating while still running the universe at the same time is enough to thank Him for all He has done. Always know that God is still in control over everything we face in our day-to-day struggles.

DAY 63

RETURN FOR A REASON

The LORD said to Moses, "When you return to Egypt, see that you perform before Pharaoh all the wonders I have given you the power to do. But I will harden his heart so that he will not let the people go.

Exodus 4:21

Doesn't it feel good to return to something that you had planned out the first time but didn't know then what you know now? When you were younger, you might have had a setback caused by rejections, delays and the incomplete discovery of your true self- identity. Now you're older, with a keen sense of wisdom, the way you move with efficiency, direction, and drive has drastically changed. You are moving in maturity instead of settling for insecurity. Now you see things well in advance before it forms into another dead end destiny. Now you know how to grab debt by the horns preventing banks from luring you back into credit card debt.

Scripture Illustration

Moses had a sense of urgency to return to Egypt. He told Jethro, the head priest of Midian, that he wanted to head back to save his people from slavery, showing them the signs God gave him as proof of God's power. Not only did Moses have a partner in his goal to tackle the mission, but he also had the faith to move out and travel in spite of God had hardening Pharaoh's heart. (Read: Exodus 4:21)

Devotional Take Away

Whatever God desires for your life, it's designed specifically for you. He might be telling you to return to the brilliant business plan you had before. He might be telling you to return to the blueprints of the nail and hair salon business you have been dreaming about. God could be pulling you back to attend seminary to be a future pastor running a ministry for the kingdom of God. God could be planning for that military recruiter to call you back to give you positive feedback from the test you took to enter the military. God could be calling you to return to law school to practice law full-time. You never know the plans God has for you until you see a sign and a vision of His power in person.

DAY 64

SIGNS & PLAGUES

Aaron threw his staff down in front of Pharaoh and his officials, and it became
a snake. Pharaoh then summoned wise men and sorcerers, and the Egyptian
magicians also did the same things by their secret arts: Each one threw down
his staff and it became a snake. But Aaron's staff swallowed up their staffs.

EXODUS 7:10-12

Trying to prove yourself over and over to gain respect from peers and friends can take years and years of "Show me proof you're the real deal." At work, your boss studies the patterns of your work ethic and efficiency. After two years of consistent, confident performance, he starts to believe in you. On the fifth year of being on the job, he promotes you to a manager. Now you see what he sees when a new kid on the block comes in as a rookie. You showed signs to prove your worth to a man, but those signs are not the real total of your worth. When you grab hold of the truth and see God reveal to you the signs of His power, life takes on greater meaning.

Scripture Illustration

The people of Egypt felt the pain of Pharaoh's no. I'm sure the Egyptians wondered why the plagues weren't affecting the children of Israel. God made the distinction between God's people and the Egyptian people. The lesson God was teaching was to be in awe of His power, regardless of whether you know the reasons for His actions or not. It feels incredible to know the reasons behind God's power. (Read: Exodus 7)

Devotional Take Away

When God gives the sign, He desires sign proof illustration of His power with the confidence of a true king running a kingdom. Always know that when it's time to prove God's power, He always confirms with a witness sign through His word and in visions. God doesn't make a fool of Himself. He knows the details before the big picture. "Knowing the end from the beginning" means more than just a sign or a miracle. God calculates His power well in advance far beyond our modern way of thinking.

DAY 65

THE CROSSOVER

Raise your staff and stretch out your hand over the sea to divide the water so that the Israelites can go through the sea on dry ground. I will harden the hearts of the Egyptians so that they will go in after them. And I will gain glory through Pharaoh and all his army, through his chariots and his horsemen.

EXODUS 14:16-17

The courage it takes to face obstacles and battles is a journey in itself. When things are going well, life feels smooth and easy. What happens when all hope breaks apart, falling into lost pieces of uncertainty? What happens when the Enemy chases the back trails of your life into a head-on collision of emotional breakdown? What do you do when you are held at gunpoint and need God to save you with praying a silent prayer under your breath? Flashbacks of where God has brought you from tend to happen in slow motion. God doesn't allow challenges to happen to waste time. He does it to help us examine our faults, weaknesses, and fears.

Scripture Illustration

The children of Israel walked many miles before crossing the Red Sea. The current depth of the Red Sea is over 7,000 feet in places. God was miraculously at work to provide safe passage for his people. Over 600,000 men (this number does not include women and children), along with cargo, livestock, food, and provisions, were all moving forward with one purpose. After crossing the Red Sea, they saw the Egyptians drown before their eyes. The very army that had enforced their slavery was now drowning in front of them. (Read: Exodus 14)

Devotional Take Away

Sometimes it may take a few more days for the scab to heal. When you rush to peel the scab of pain, you delay what God is trying to heal you from. Let's stop provoking the pain and walk through the sea on dry land. We might have to walk for eight hours with weighty issues of baggage before God takes them away. This walking process could produce a hidden healing in the middle of the sea your facing now.

DAY 66

BITTER EXCUSES

When they came to Marah, they could not drink its water because
it was bitter. (That is why the place is called Marah.) So the people
grumbled against Moses, saying, "What are we to drink?"

EXODUS 15:23-24

Christina lives with her family in a small village in Ghana, West Africa. The country is so close to the equator that rain rarely falls in a year. Every year up to eight months can go by without rainfall. The small pond that Christina's family relies on every day slowly dries up with the heat and evaporation from the sun. Sometimes Christina walks so far for water that she doesn't make it back in time to attend school. She is the only hope for her parents. Both parents are suffering from infections and issues caused by unclean water. She is the last resort for mobility, energy, and strength to find water.

Scripture Illustration

In the Scripture, we see that the children of Israel were already complaining about bitter water before they had traveled roughly three days in a desert called Shur. For a short time, they thought the water was just around the corner. After arriving at Marah, they noticed that the water was bitter. They began throwing a complaining fit to Moses, saying, "How in the world are we going to drink this water when it's completely bitter?" Moses cried out to the Lord, asking for help and instruction. God gave the instruction: "If you listen to Me closely and follow my instructions, I will not bring diseases on you as I did with the Egyptians." (Read: Exodus 15)

Devotional Take Away

Even when the water runs dry and your thirst for God is wavering with the same distractions of fear and doubt remember that God could be using the circumstances as a measuring faith tool to see if you trust Him with nothing. We are called to be faithful stewards in the kingdom of God. We might not always have access to messages of hope every Sunday and Wednesday, but we can still have hope for tomorrow. When you live on the wings of hope, your response to God doesn't include bitter excuses. Are you thirsty for God or for the natural things you have easy access to?

DAY 67

LEFTOVERS

*When the dew was gone, thin flakes like frost on the ground appeared
on the desert floor. When the Israelites saw it, they said to each
other, "What is it?" For they did not know what it was.*

Exodus 16:14-15

Five more days, until the direct deposit clears with only $16.87 left in the checking account the only thing left to hold onto, is a wing and a prayer. The refrigerator's empty, and the car battery is completely dead. The job is only part-time, paying barely enough to cover all of the bills. The gas needle is so close to empty that there is no possible way to attempt a one-way ride to the nearest gas station. Then God sends an angel in the flesh with a seed offering so great that you have leftovers from the increase. God instructs you to bless someone with your increase; instead, you use it for personal use and pleasure.

Scripture Illustration

The children of Israel complained over and over to Moses, begging for food to eat. They wanted a temporary fix to balance their lack of belief in God. God had proved Himself over and over, but doubt entered the minds of the people. They reverted to the defeated, broken mentality that had kept them enslaved in Egypt, but God showed His power yet another time. They enjoyed a meal of quail, followed by manna, a honey wafer that appeared like frost on the ground. As they ate, they were satisfied. Moses told them not to save any. He knew that if the people tried to save the manna, it would rot and spoil. (Read: Exodus 16)

Devotional Take Away

God can bless you so much that the leftovers have a story to tell. The overflow of leftovers can be so high that it hurts the overall vision and intent of the sign. The overflow can promote gluttony, excess, and addictions. A journey of giving can keep you from getting sick. Think about focusing on the change within the change knowing that God is the central source of the change. Having extra to give to someone in need feels a lot better than buying what we don't need.

DAY 68

⟨⟩⟨⟩⟨⟩⟨⟩⟨⟩⟨⟩⟨⟩

HEAVY HANDS

When Moses' hands grew tired, they took a stone and put it under Him and he sat on it. Aaron and Hur held his hands up--one on one side, and one on the other--so that this hands remained steady till sunset. So Joshua overcame the Amalekite army with the sword.

Exodus 17:12-13

When the hand of God orchestrates the pathway of your life, neither age, income, nor distance matters when it comes to completing the assignment. God knows the ones He chooses and calls them from birth. God never makes mistakes. What appears to be a mistake is God's tool to teach us how He thinks. You may be in a situation where a friend or family member is needed to lift your hands to defeat the Enemy. When your hands are down, the temptation to quit and die feels easy.

Scripture Illustration

Moses was feeling the weight of old age. He knew the Amalekites were coming to attack at Rephidim, so he gave instructions to Joshua, telling him to find the best men from the tribes to fight against the Amalekites. Moses planned to head to the top of the hill and stand with his staff and his hands raised while Joshua and his men fought the Amalekites. Moses noticed a difference when his hands were raised compared to when they were down. Every time he would drop his hand, the Amalekites started winning the battle. The momentum of the battle shifted as the power of God was in the winning hands of a chosen people. (Read: Exodus 17)

Devotional Take Away

I'm a living witness that difficult times in life hurt the most when so-called friends make the same excuses for not begin there for you based on irony of introverted thinking. If you can find at least two good friends that you trust as great examples of Godly peers, you can win battles and victories against your opposition. There is nothing like having a friend on your left and right when you need them there. His perspective and focus never drys out. His initial goal is to break down the cracks and open spaces of your spiritual armor. What you think is tough is a piece of cake to the Devil. He loves to magnify things to extreme emotional levels. With God on our side, we know that our strength is unmatched by a person, battleground, or obstacles we may be facing.

EXECUTIVE ORDER

When the people saw the thunder and lightning and heard the trumpet, and saw the mountain in smoke, they trembled with fear. They stayed at a distance.

EXODUS 20:18

As the world witnessed the first ten days of Donald J. Trump's presidency with the signing and confirming of twelve executive orders, America shifted into an outcry of anger and division. An executive order imposed a 120-day suspension of the refugee program and a 90-day ban on travel to the U.S. from citizens of seven terror hot spots: Iraq, Iran, Syria, Libya, Yemen, Somalia, and Sudan. Millions of women marched in protest, expressing unequal conditions in the workplace.

Scripture Illustration

The people said to Moses, "If you speak to us, we will listen, but do not let God speak with us, lest we die." As God was giving the ten commandments, lightning and thunder accentuated the power of God's voice. The people were shocked to the point that they asked Moses to tell God to stop speaking. When the power of God feels fearful, the act of reverence to authority covers everything in its pathway. The children of Israel feared the outcome of the meeting God had with Moses on the mountain. (Read: Exodus 20)

Devotional Take Away

1. Thou shall not worship other gods (When you worship anything, that takes the attention off of God. You have put something in place of God's power). 2. Thou shall not make idols of any kind (statues of other gods or material things that displace the deity of God). 3. You are to keep God's name holy and not misuse it (cursing or using the Lord's name in vain when you feel frustrated or angry) 4. You are not to work on the Sabbath; instead, keep it holy (filling your time by working on business-related contracts in place of Sunday morning worship). 5. Honor your parents so that you live long on the earth (take time to go the extra mile with any additional errands and needs they might desire). 6. You are not to murder. 7. You are not to commit adultery 8. You are not to steal 9. You are not to lie 10. You are not to desire anything that belongs to someone else.

DAY 70

NAIVE WORSHIPERS

And he took the calf the people had made and burned it in the fire; then he
ground it to powder, scattered it on the water and made the Israelites drink it.

EXODUS 32:20

Have you been to a worship service where you walked in for the first time as a visitor and immediately noticed the body language of the people who were supposed to be worshiping God? Some had disgusted looks on their faces, with arms crossed, sleepy eyes, and unwelcoming characteristics. Then you see the "going through the motions worshiper" that is putting up with the songs by substituting random boring thoughts. Then you notice the "I went to the club last night" worshiper who jumps and shouts for attention, wanting to be seen. I call these the "naive worshipers." Their belief system lacks real value numbing their reverence and worship to God. They no longer can tell the difference between a fake worship encounter and a God-breathed encounter that shakes the core of the heart.

Scripture Illustration

The people said, "We need something to see and worship. Moses is taking too long on the mountain, so we need something made from our gold and jewelry to worship." Aaron became the accomplice of the people as he gathered every form of gold they presented. Aaron placed the gold in the fire, melting and shaping the gold into a calf. The people cheered, "God wasn't the one who led us out. This golden calf was the reason we were able to leave Egypt." (Read: Exodus 32)

Devotional Take Away

The more you learn about the things of God, the more God reveals the hidden treasure of true worship. Give Him all the glory even when your emotions don't make sense. God is longing for the lost time you miss during the mid work weeks of your schedule. When you yield to Him in a fresh, comprehensive way, the subtle moments of Grace will start to guide you through the chaos. God flexes His muscles when you give you all at the altar. Let's show God the true essence of how we worship Him. He deserves our best worship, our best praise and our best offering.

DAY 71

BUILT TO LAST

All those who were skilled among the workers made the tabernacle
with ten curtains of finely twisted linen and blue, purple and scarlet
yarn, with cherubim woven into them by expert hands. All the curtains
were the same size twenty-eight cubits long and four cubits wide.

EXODUS 36:8-9

Apple technology is known for excellence, brilliance, pioneering and innovation. From software developers and "genius bar" support specialists, Apple lives to inspire generations of customers who believe and respect great technology. At times, leaks display versions of a product like the iPhone that we never see released. Many times these leaks come from China, where a factory worker has been paid to hand off a prototype to a blogger or journalist. It turns out that once Apple is done building a product, it redesigns the product and sends it through the manufacturing process again, explaining the various versions we may see leaked. This process lasts 4-6 weeks and ends with a gathering of responsible Apple employees at the factory.

Scripture Illustration

The children of Israel were assigned various tasks based on their talent and efficiency. From twisted linen to scarlet yarn and cherubim's interwoven into the curtains by the hands of the best experts, God gave Moses direction to form the best team for the design of the tabernacle. Even with the ark of the covenant, Moses used the expertise of Bezalel, a highly skilled craftsman. He layered the ark with gold in the interior and even on the exterior of the ark. The cover, acacia wood poles, cherubim wings, and other details to the ark reflected the design and detail of the tabernacle. (Read: Exodus 26)

Devotional Take Away

God has given us the ability to live and move in the spirit of excellence. Excellence provides specific designs for specific needs. When God lays out the blueprint design as a prototype, He uses visions to work out His desires and plans for our lives. He desires the best and knows which capacity we can handle. He knows that our gifts and talents are valuable enough to get the job done for the kingdom of God.

DAY 72

WRONG KIND OF FIRE

Aaron's sons Nadab and Abihu took their censers, put fire in them and
added incense; and they offered unauthorized fire before the LORD,
contrary to his command. So fire came out from the presence of the
LORD and consumed them, and they died before the LORD.

LEVITICUS 10:1-2

Cooking foods with the wrong type of oil can be the downfall of a great meal. If you toss frozen fried foods into hot oil, you're asking for an instant fire to happen with skin blisters. Certain things take a half an hour to thaw out before cooking preparations begin. Even when food is thawed, it's always smart to use a paper towel to dab any remaining wetness before frying. This protocol is basic cooking knowledge that a well-seasoned cook understands from experience.

Scripture Illustration

In this story, Aaron was the high priest in charge of the protocol of the tabernacle. Aaron's two sons, Nadab and Abihu, offered up strange burnt offerings contrary to what God had instructed. The Bible says that as they approached the altar, the Lord struck them with a fire that blazed out from the altar, consuming their flesh. The puzzling part about this transition is that Aaron couldn't mourn the death of his sons because he was consecrated with oil and set apart from the guilt and sin his sons had brought into the camp. (Read: Leviticus 10)

Devotional Take Away

The outcome of God's wrath can grab the attention of the disobedient. Operating with the wrong kind of fire brings torment, misunderstanding, frustration, stress, and confusion. Wasted with the wrong sacrifice, God reacts with power and stern action. When God makes things sacred, He requires a unique kind of protocol. What we do behind closed doors is never hidden from God. When we try to offer up half-hearted worship, He can tell when it's scripted and rehearsed. When it's dead, He knows, and when it feels overdone without substance, He still knows. The things we offer should be what the Lord truly wants from our lives. He rewards sincere worship with an open heart of adoration.

STUCK BETWEEN TEETH

But while the meat was still between their teeth and before it could be consumed, the anger of the LORD burned against the people, and he struck them with a severe plague.

NUMBERS 11:33

Two spoiled sons from a wealthy neighborhood have been living with their parents for a long time. One is twenty-eight, and the other is thirty. They choose not to work for themselves, and they choose not to apply for jobs online. Both parents had bailed them out, paying their expenses when they were in and out of prison three times for the same misdemeanor. The parents are tired of babysitting and nursing grown men. They're tired of hearing the same excuses. These sons eat at their parents' table for free; they don't buy any groceries but sit there with meat stuck between their teeth.

Scripture Illustration

Moses said to God, "Why do I have to nurse their issues as if I were their mother?" Moses was distraught over the fact that the Israelites didn't appreciate what he did for them. God perform repeated many times over proving God's power and wonder, but the children of Israel still didn't get it. They were selfish, impatient, lazy, and demanding. The children of Israel were long overdue for severe judgment. They lost appreciation for God's power, and they lost the faith to endure beyond the current condition. (Read: Numbers 11)

Devotional Take Away

God knows that when we give up and return to the things He delivered us from, it's ten times harder to bounce back because of our past failures. The meat is still stuck in the teeth of low self-esteem, anger, doubt, oppression, anxiety, division, unbelief, covetousness, and sexual immorality. God uses His scale of accountability knowing that we are prone to falling short of his glory. He can sense the preconceived games we play when no one is watching. God is aware of the sham and phony facade behind the church mask. He sees right through the meat on the bone. The decisions we make and the results of how we view and appreciate God must come from a dedicated, open love His grace and provision.

DAY 74

WATCH YOUR MOUTH

*Miriam and Aaron began to talk against Moses because of his Cushite wife,
for he had married a Cushite. "Has the LORD spoken only through Moses?"
they asked. "Hasn't he also spoken through us?" And the LORD heard this.*

NUMBERS 12:1-2

Gossipers always feel that they can say what they want, how they want, and when they want. People irritated with unresolved insecurity issues speak from independent spheres of low self-esteem. Most people with this problem might have slipped on black ice a few times without proper mentorship, spiritual covering, and follow-up. People bash texting in and out of church is similar to gossiping and laughing right in someone's face in public. Believers must hold the people in our circles accountable when they choose to gossip about men and women of God. We must protect the anointing and dignity of great spiritual leaders.

Scripture Illustration

Moses married a Cushite (Ethiopian) woman later in his life. During this transition time, Miriam and Aaron started gossiping and questioning Moses's thought processes. They were downgrading the fact that he was listening to and hearing from God. Their sarcasm flared up with the question, "Has he not spoken through us also?" God heard their words and was heated and had to do something. He began to define Moses's position and protect Moses's authority by telling Miriam and Aaron to come to the tent of meeting and to stand at the entrance in the presence of the Lord. God decided to take another route, giving Miriam leprosy and causing her skin to be pale white. (Read: Numbers 12)

Devotional Take Away

God has not forgotten your prayers, nor is He hard of hearing. He will be God until the end of time. When He speaks, the mountains shake, and when He reveals Himself, men stand at attention in fear and reverence of His power. The face of God is so bright that it would bring blindness if you were to look at His face directly. We serve a mighty God who loves and protects our sanity and dignity.

DAY 75

DODGING COURAGE

Why is the LORD bringing us to this land only to let us fall by the sword? Our wives and our children will be taken as plunder. Wouldn't it be better for us to go back to Egypt?" And they said to each other, "We should choose a leader and go back to Egypt."

NUMBERS 14:3

A soldier in the US Army has requirements to fulfill after taking the oath to serve in the armed forces. When soldiers, sailors, and national guardsmen verbally affirm their dedication to being a real soldier, things must change. All the games, childish responses, and prearranged excuses go out the window. If a soldier rejects battle when asked to go to the front line, he's viewed as a coward for two reasons. The first reason is he said no, secondly because he went back on his word concerning the code of conduct. The commander handles such issues by processing the soldier's dishonorable discharge without benefits and showing him the exit door.

Scripture Illustration

Moses gives the go-ahead to Joshua, Caleb, and the other ten spies to survey the land for its goods and resources. Some returned after forty days with large grape clusters on poles, saying that the city walls were tremendous and the people were intimidating. Joshua and Caleb returned from their spy journey saying, "Look, we can turn up the conquest; we've got this. God can give us the victory in this battle, and we can take the land." The other ten spies said, "No, we can't do this. We are out-numbered, small, and like grasshoppers compared to the enemies we are facing." Joshua and Caleb came back again, making an effort to motivate the people, but the people became angry and attacked Joshua and Caleb. (Read: Numbers 14)

Devotional Take Away

When you operate behind the walls and curtains of pride, it takes a long uphill climb to get to where God desires you to be. When you attempt to fight the Enemy without God's help, the stress of losing out on opportunities will bring you to a screeching halt. It's important to know what God is in and what He is clearly is not in. Fighting battles in vain is a waste of time.

DAY 76

THE ANSWER FOR PRIDE

"But if the LORD brings about something totally new, and the earth opens its mouth and swallows them, with everything that belongs to them, and they go down alive into the realm of the dead, then you will know that these men have treated the LORD with contempt."

NUMBERS 16:30

When someone justifies their right to take on a leadership role, demanding the outcome right away without God's confirmation, raises opposition and suspicion. Over the years I've witnessed direct pride, anger, and outbursts that taught me how to manage my emotions. Church founders and leaders in the local church include senior elders, senior ministers, and well-spoken pastors. Operational leaders, team-building leaders, relationship leaders, and lastly directional leaders all play a significant role in the kingdom God.

Scripture Illustration

A man by the name of Korah was a wealthy congregational leader of the Levites. He wanted the position of the high priest with attention, honor, and power for his work. He felt entitled to the opinion of control because of his bloodline. Korah went to the children of Israel to try to sway them and change their beliefs, forming a campaign team of two hundred fifty men. These men wanted power as well. Moses and Aaron admonished the children of Israel to separate themselves from the company of Korah and his men. While Moses was warning the people, the ground began to shake, and the earth opened up and swallowed Korah, his family, Dathan, and Abiram. The other 250 leaders were struck down and killed by fire. (Read: Numbers 16)

Devotional Take Away

The answer God provides is not always the answer we may be expecting. God sometimes works to construct the strangest occurrences with unpredicted results. If you spend time with rebels, cheaters, complainers, and drunkards, you'll start living and thinking like them. The Enemy uses frustration as a gateway to disable your identity and dreams. Take control before it turns into a life or death situation.

SNAKE BITE

Pray that the Lord will take the snakes away from us." So Moses prayed for the people. The LORD said to Moses, "Make a snake and put it up on a pole." Then when anyone was bitten by a snake and looked at the bronze snake, they lived.

NUMBERS 21:7-8

A seminary professor asked a student to write a paper on a specific biblical topic based on storylines assigned. The student persevered through long nights of studying. At times he would fall asleep in the middle of his study time. After days and days of research and hard work, he turned in the paper to the teacher. The teacher returned his essay with a considerable F written in red ink. The student was in shock, frustrated and concerned about the reason why. He asked "How can you do this to me? I worked so hard on this paper. I went to the library and checked out the best books that fit my topic." The professor said, "There is no question that you worked hard, putting great effort into the paper of your interest, but I'm afraid this wasn't the assignment."

Scripture Illustration

God gave Moses the instruction to speak to the rock. "Take the staff and assemble the congregation, you and Aaron your brother. Before their eyes, tell the rock to yield its water. So you shall bring water out of the rock for them and give drink to the congregation and their cattle. Moses was acting out of frustration and hatred because of the rebellion of the Israelites. His response was to give them a bit of his anger mixed with a "Take this water since you want it bad enough" attitude. (Read: Numbers 21)

Devotional Take Away

Frustration and complaining causes long-lasting pain of incomplete goals. How many have times have we played the frustration role with God to the point that we never reach the Promised Land of our desires. We need a few wake-up snake bites to get our attention and remind us that God is still God. When God unleashes his wrath, there is no running from the heat. One text message, one phone call, or even a night out with friends can get God into a heated discussion concerning our obedience to Him.

DAY 78

THE HIRED CURSE

They came to Balaam and said: "This is what Balak son of Zippor says: Do not let anything keep you from coming to me, because I will reward you handsomely and do whatever you say. Come and put a curse on these people for me."

NUMBERS 22:16-17

Many people in our current culture use bribes of wealth and fame to obtain what they want. A Las Vegas casino owner may advertise his brand by saying, "If you come to my casino and gamble at the slot machines, you will get not only free drinks but also free food all night. If you purchase the VIP pass, you will be given a celebrity backstage pass to get autographs and pictures." The gullible customer that barely has enough money to enjoy his or her trip for a week blows the cash in three days. The next morning the same customer wakes up with a mean hangover, not remembering what happened. He checks his bank account balance, feeling cursed and robbed by people he doesn't even know.

Scripture Illustration

King Balak of Moab is determined to offer the most significant possible bribe to manipulate the prophet Balaam to curse the Israelites. Balaam told the Moabites and Midianites to stay the night so that he could find out what the Lord would say. Balaam undoubtedly didn't rush God's answer, despite the riches, gold, and gifts offered by the king. Balaam told the servants of King Balak to return to their king. The king sent men a second time with double the riches. The second time God granted Balaam to go, saying, "Only go when I say go and do as I say do." God set Balaam up to test the direction of his heart. (Read: Numbers 22)

Devotional Take Away

You might be great at something that fits the bill of compensation. Before accepting the offer, seek God's offer first. You may be gifted and talented in the eyes of man, but in the eyes of God, you're just a speck in His infinite eternity. He is the God of interruptions and the God of great answers. God loves when we seek Him first even before and after the deal.

DAY 79

HARLOTS IN THE CAMP

While Israel was staying in Shittim, the men began to indulge in sexual immorality with Moabite women, who invited them to the sacrifices to their gods. The people ate the sacrificial meal and bowed down before these gods.

NUMBERS 25:1-2

Wild, late-night parties, orgies, drug use, hangovers, fights, and prostitution run heavy in the streets of every state and country around the world. At first, such a life appears enjoyable. On the dance floor, the music is playing, and everyone is in a trance, thinking everything is cool. All of a sudden, a random person comes out of nowhere and says, "We have a VIP party upstairs. Come join us." When you walk upstairs to the VIP party, you find that the private room is filled with cocaine, ecstasy pills, weed, and free alcohol. What looks like a great time is a room filled with more profound issues of insecurity, pain, and random acts of sexual thrills, not to mention the sexually transmitted diseases that no one wants to confess to but continue to be spread to others.

Scripture Illustration

God was furious! He sent a plague, and 24,000 people died. One of the Israelites brought a Midianite woman to his family tent. They walked right past Moses and the elders of Israel. The son of the high priest took a spear and went into the tent. He thrust the spear through them both, killing them on the spot. After the spear went through them both, the curse was lifted from off the camp. With that action, God stopped the plague. (Read: Numbers 25)

Devotional Take Away

How many times have you felt wrong about a weekend that ended in a hangover of depression? Somehow you found a way to get up and go to church, but when the preacher was speaking, you were thinking, God, why do I feel like he is talking directly to me? God, why do I feel weighed down by past failures that keep me from moving forward in life. God, I should know better by now. When you know who you are and whose you are, the vision and focus of your purpose pushes you to the next level of destiny.

DAY 80

THE G.O.A.T

For no one has ever shown the mighty power or performed the
awesome deeds that Moses did in the sight of all Israel.

DEUTERONOMY 34:12

America witnessed one of the greatest comebacks in Super Bowl history when the New England Patriots received their fifth Super Bowl trophy by beating the Atlanta Falcons in a jaw-dropping, overtime comeback win. The quarterback for the Patriots, Tom Brady, became the G.O.A.T. that day. When I was growing up, my friends in school would call the best player at the top of the game, with stats to prove it, the G.O.A.T. (Greatest of All Time/ GOAT). Michael Jordan, Muhammad Ali, Tiger Woods, Serena Williams, Usain Bolt, and now Tom Brady has made the list of greatest players of all time.

Scripture Illustration

The same impact and influence were witnessed in the life of Moses. Moses was considered the G.O.A.T of his day. When the Israelites needed a hero, they depended on Moses to get them from point A to point B. Consider the miracles Moses performed after God gave him his assignment to free the children of Israel from slavery: Under God's direction, Moses' rod turned into a serpent (Exodus 7:10),the water of the river became blood (Exodus 7:17), a plague of frogs appeared (Exodus 8:2), Moses smote the dust of the earth, turning it to lice (Exodus 8:17), a grievous plague fell upon the Egyptians' cattle (Exodus 9:3), the Egyptians were smitten with boils (Exodus 9:9), a hailstorm devastated the land (Exodus 9:18), the plague of locusts covered all of Egypt (Exodus 10:14), darkness fell across the land of Egypt for three days (Exodus 10:22)

Devotional Take Away

With God's power, there is still a hero inside of you. God knows that your calling is the answer to your financial freedom and security. You have tried almost every job possible, but for some reason, they never seem to work out. God shuts down the momentum and potential job security to help you increase your spiritual wisdom and safety. You have the drive, strength, an advantage to be the best God has called you to be.

DAY 81

INSURED PROTECTION

(But she had taken them up to the roof and hidden them under the stalks of flax she had laid out on the roof.) So the men set out in pursuit of the spies on the road that leads to the fords of the Jordan, and as soon as the pursuers had gone out, the gate was shut.

JOSHUA 2:6-7

Texas has some of their worst hail storms in the first three months of the year. Insurance companies are bombarded with large numbers of claims for roof damage due to hail and wind damage during these months. When a hail storm happens, it doesn't matter how sturdy the foundation under the roof is. The wind can still blow the underlayment and shingles entirely off the roof. Having coverage under a particular insurance plan covers what they can afford.

Scripture Illustration

The Bible says that Rahab became an accomplice for two of Joshua's men who were spies. Rahab, the harlot, wasn't just another harlot; she was a smart harlot. She knew the city would collapse as a result of anger, war, and power. What better way to save herself and others in her family. When she hid the two men between the stalks of flax on the roof, their lives were saved. The soldiers came into Rahab's living quarters and asked, "Have you seen two men? They are spying on the city and plan to send word to kill us. We couldn't find them, so they must be here somewhere. Any idea where they might be?" (Read Joshua 2:)

Devotional Take Away

We will never break the code of God's insurance plan, but what we do know is to give Him the honor and praise He deserves for being God. The fact that our protection extends beyond the walls of adversity is enough to believe still that God will make a way. God works in ways that feel unchurch and unorthodox. God has our purpose and plan in the palm of His hand, waiting for us to yield and open up to Him. The conditions we face day after day, month after month, year after year are second and third chances God needs to see before He gives us the reward and victory.

DAY 82

NO WET FEET

Yet as soon as the priests who carried the ark reached the Jordan and their feet touched the water's edge, the water from upstream stopped flowing.

JOSHUA 3:15

The term "getting your feet wet" is one of the oldest clichés. This phrase can refer to experiencing something for the first time, taking a risk, or learning something new. You might hear this phrase if you are watching a new hiring manager conduct on-the-job training for new employees. At times, new beginnings can become burdensome. Weighing the parameters of untouched opportunity can boost a different kind of moral and identity. Some people get their feet wet in modern churches, schools, work environments, or various social settings. However, you go about getting your feet wet, make sure you understand the teachings involved in the process.

Scripture Illustration

Joshua gave instructions for the priest to bring the ark of the covenant to the Jordan River. As they approached, their feet felt a bit wet. The river strangely stopped flowing and became still. From this moment forward, the people knew that God's presence was with Joshua as it had been with Moses. As the wall of water formed, flowing in the power of God the people were reminded of Gods greatness. Seeing this, the priests walked to the middle of the riverbed and stood on dry ground. Then the people started moving across the river. (Read: Joshua 3)

Devotional Take Away

Some of you have seen the hand of God in the lives of your parents, friends, and family many times before; I believe God is shifting the torch into your hands. God has it covered when you think the bottom has fallen out of every one of your opportunities and dreams. He has it covered when the family argument at the dinner table turns violent to the point of no one talking to each other for a month. God has it covered when a late bill fee pops up just when you think your credit score is improving. God has it included when you discover that you need a check-up for cancer-related symptoms. If He did it before, H\\will find a way to do it again. Trust in God, pray hard, and watch the power of the Lord reveal His strength and promise for your life.

SHOUT UNTILL IN FALLS

*When you hear them sound a long blast on the trumpets, have
the whole army give a loud shout; then the wall of the city will
collapse and the army will go up, everyone straight in.*

JOSHUA 6:5

When someone shouts, regardless of the situation, the sense of power behind the roar delivers a meaning. When a man is harassing a woman in front of a large group of people, and she shouts, "STOP! YOU'RE HARASSING ME!" it not only gets the attention of the crowd, but it embarrasses the man to the point that he feels the need to back off and stop immediately. Men get nervous when embarrassment grabs a hold of there intentions to do wrong.

Scripture Illustration

Joshua arranged seven priests who were to blow ram-horn trumpets. The ark of God was behind them, and the rest of the army followed the ark. Joshua told the people, "Don't say one word as you march around the city." He gave them the additional instruction to wait for his call to shout on the seventh day of marching. Joshua told the people that after shouting, they were to completely wipe out the city, leaving only Rahab and her family alive. When the people shouted, the walls began to shake, with the city gates and walls collapsing in a domino effect. (Read Joshua 6:5)

Devotional Take Away

The victory God is about to give you will require that you shout it into reality. God isn't just going to hand this to you; it's going to take a war cry—a cry of sincere adoration and worship. God is so strategic that He has certain types of yells, cries, and shouts that get His attention. Anybody can yell "JESUS." The difference is a true connection, and a cry for help is not granted a response unless you believe and declare that there is no other name greater than the name of Jesus. When you are in desperate need to be saved, God will hear you when you "shout it out" with all your heart. Keep shouting, keep praying and fasting God hears the cries of the ones that diligently seek Him. Sometimes you have to shout until it breaks.

DAY 84

WHAT'S IN THE TENT?

*Achan replied, "It is true! I have sinned against the LORD, the God
of Israel. This is what I have done: When I saw in the plunder a
beautiful robe from Babylonia, two hundred shekels of silver and a
bar of gold weighing fifty shekels, I coveted them and took them.*

JOSHUA 7:20-21

Some of you have hidden secrets that only God knows. The same repeated sin
has crippled your walk with God. Deep down in your heart, you know that if it
weren't for God's grace, you wouldn't be alive to tell the story. The level of belief
expected to be carried out is a lot different today. We tend to get away with more
without any apparent consequences. Back in Bible days, His judgment was more
swift and life-threatening. However, God still sees what is hidden, what needs
to be confessed. Confess whatever needs to be cleansed and let God deal with
the issue.

Scripture Illustration

Achan knew that what he had done was against God's standard for every
tribe. The measure was so high regarding not taking the spoils from the battle
that it meant death if someone was caught. Joshua had to expose the rotten
apple in the camp to save the lives of his people. God told Joshua, "If you don't
handle this, the guilt and sin will be on everyone." God was holding every tribe
accountable, even for the hidden, unknown mistake of a friend or family member.
Achan admitted what he had done. "I took 200 pieces of silver, a gold bar, and a
coat from Babylon and placed them in my tent." Joshua took Achan, his wife, his
children, his livestock, his tent, and everything he had stolen and burned them
in front of all of the tribes for everyone to see. (Read Joshua 7:20-21)

Devotional Take Away

The next time you pray to God, knowing that you haven't acknowledged
your unconfessed sins, catch yourself and pause for a minute. Let Him hear your
confession from your mouth so you can know in your heart that your guilt is
gone and so you can avoid the sinful lifestyle of mundane Christianity. He is an
all-hearing God who is willing to forgive you when you miss the mark.

DAY 85

OVERLOOKED

They put worn and patched sandals on their feet and wore old clothes. All the bread of their food supply was dry and moldy.

JOSHUA 9:3-5

What appears to be legit and pleasant on the surface could be the very thing that is deceiving you. The dangers associated with commercials for performance-enhancing drugs on TV are often overlooked. The commercial starts out glamorous, with a couple running in the park with clean hair, clean shoes, and well-made clothes. What you may not notice are the small black letters at the bottom of the screen, stating that there could be serious side effects: migraines, excessive coughing, diarrhea, vomiting, rashes, and muscle fatigue.

Scripture Illustration

When the Gibeonites thought up the idea to use old garments, torn clothing, wore-down shoes, molded bread, and old wineskins, they thought the deception was brilliant. They assumed that the Israelites were trying to kill them and take over the land. So why not? Joshua asked their country of origin, and they lied, saying they lived very far away. The real story was that the Gibeonites were a physically strong but mentally weak group of people. They feared the Israelites to the point that they set up a treaty with Joshua out of deception. (Read: Joshua 9)

Devotional Take Way

God allows no make-up, no filter, no holiday mask when He is working in your favor to fight the tactics of the Enemy. If you ask for more time to fight, God will begin to move based on confession. Scenarios can stand still like the mannequin challenge when God is on your side. The prayers of the righteous are more than enough. We need the kind of boldness that is so stirring that God will follow our words of obedience and flip the situation to His power and glory. Being half-way in and half-way out makes the heart weighed down by false happiness. It's time for God to raise up a generation that will "Go ye therefore, and teach all nations, baptizing them in the name of the Father, and of the Son, and of the Holy Ghost" (Matthew 28:19, KJV).

DAY 86

FASCINATED BY GREATNESS

"Behold this stone will be a witness against us. It has heard all the words the LORD has said to us. It will be a witness against you if you are untrue to your God." Then Joshua dismissed the people, each to their own inheritance.

JOSHUA 24:-27

When greatness is witnessed over and over, it's hard to put your finger on how God uses people with such a fantastic gift that goes beyond words. Some of you reading this now have looked up to your favorite athletes, actors, doctors, preachers, musicians, presidents, investors, or business owners. What you saw in them is defined as a natural attraction to success or greatness. I remember watching Benny Hinn and being fascinated by Kathryn Kuhlman's preaching and miracle crusades. I also remember watching Kobe Bryant studying Michael Jordan on the court when he first came into the league. I can remember watching Steven Young review the playbooks after watching Joe Montana play some of the greatest games of his career. Everyone has a hero. Being in awe of the talent someone has can provoke a deeper hunger to step up your game and be the most significant person you can be.

Scripture Illustration

From the killing of five kings to the battles of Ai and Jericho, God stayed with Joshua the entire time. The parting of the Jordan River, the rubble of the walls of Jericho, and the protection of the ark of the covenant were all a part of the greatness of Joshua, even in between battles. Joshua saved Rahab's family but also received instructions to take out Achan's family. He slipped in the lure of the Gibeonites' manipulation but used the experience as a teaching tool to gain wisdom. (Read: Joshua:24)

Devotional Take Away

The Enemy loves to disconnect the mind, causing isolation to the point of loneliness and destroying ambition. It's time to think and strategize beyond the applause. After the Sunday message is over think about how far God has brought you from. Even before you get to the church parking lot as you ponder thoughts in between traffic lights consider God's greatness and plan He has for your life. It's worth pausing and reflecting on His goodness.

DAY 87

SOUTH PAW

And Ehud came to him as he was sitting alone in his cool roof
chamber. And Ehud said, "I have a message from God for you." And
he arose from his seat. And Ehud reached with his left hand, took
the sword from his right thigh, and thrust it into his belly.

JUDGES 3:20-21

The phrase "southpaw" is a boxing slang term for a left-handed boxer. Sometimes coaches say that person is a "lefty." The advantages of a left-handed boxer can throw a right-handed fighter off guard if the technique is carried out correctly. A left-handed boxer can start off jabbing with his left and then throw a power punch with his right to make it seem that he's right-handed. He also can switch up styles and reverse the fighting pattern to give his opponent a different kind of challenge.

Scripture Illustration

At this time in history, King Eglon, king of Moab, was killing, ruling, and demanding complete control over the Israelites. For eighteen years, King Eglon had terrorized the children of Israel. King Eglon was an obese man. He would eat so much that he needed assistance from his servants to get him from point A to point B. Ehud was tired of watching his family and fellow tribe members live in fear of what the king was doing to the children of Israel. (Read: Judges 3:20-21)

Devotional Take Away

God may be switching up hands to show you what He has in store for your destiny, perhaps for your career or another opportunity. The battle is far from over. You have too many people counting on you not to give up. You have people who believe in you and desire the best that God has planned for your life. You may possess the secret that can shock the Enemy into defeat. Not only will you be able to defeat the Enemy, but you will also lock the door so that the Enemy's associates can't enter until you're ready to set up the ambush of victory. There is a group of left-handed believers who are willing to take the call to do great things for the kingdom of God. God has given you a strategy to conquer every spiritual and physical war the Enemy wages against you.

DAY 88

LADIES FIRST

She sent and summoned Barak the son of Abinoam from Kedesh-naphtali and said to him, "Has not the Lord, the God of Israel, commanded you, 'Go, gather your men at Mount Tabor, taking 10,000 from the people of Naphtali and the people of Zebulun.

JUDGES 4:6-7

When a woman of God stands up and takes the lead, nothing can stop her. Women who provide for their families leave no stone unturned. The power of a woman's courage goes so much further than the doors and walls of the house in which she is raising her family. There is a controversy concerning a woman in the pulpit. Female bishops, pastors, elders, and ministers have endured a catalyst of repeated judgment for taking on the assignment and call of God. In the generation in which we live, the shift is toward acceptance. A woman can be just as gifted in ministry as men are.

Scripture Illustration

Deborah was the only prophetess mentioned in the Bible. She was so gifted that she had a palm tree named after her: the palm tree of Deborah. She handled the complaints and issues of the people as she sat under that tree. God's hand was on Deborah, and the people knew it. One day she called for a man named Barak and said to him, "The Lord has a message for you. He says, 'Take 10,000 men and go to Mount Tabor.'" When Barak and his men faced the Canaanite army, the commander Sisera ran when he noticed that the battle was favoring the Lord. Sisera ran to the tent of Jael, a woman married to a man who was at peace with Sisera and his army. (Read: Judges 4)

Devotional Take Away

Some women are widows, or separated, or divorced, and only God holds the clay of their life together. Some women have just been released from rehab because of drug addiction, but they are now ready to walk completely under God's direction and find shelter under His wings. Some women have been in prison for years, thinking that life is worthless. "Why am I still in this stupid prison just waiting to die?" The weight of what you are currently carrying is based on how you view it. God has the power to comfort you even in your deepest fear.

MAKE IT DEW WHAT IT DO

behold, I am laying a fleece of wool on the threshing floor. If there is dew on the fleece alone, and it is dry on all the ground, then I shall know that you will save Israel by my hand, as you have said." And it was so. When he rose early next morning and squeezed the fleece, he wrung enough dew from the fleece to fill a bowl with water.

JUDGES 6:37-38

When a younger brother watched his older brother do something mind-blowing, he became fascinated and impressed. A few seconds after the demonstration was done, the younger brother said, "Hey, that was cool. Do it again." The older brother proved that it wasn't just luck; he successfully repeated the move just like the first time. The boy clapped, yelled, and jumped with excitement, wishing to do what his brother had just done.

Scripture Illustration

Gideon was so oppressed by the Midianites that he feared what they would do next. The Midianites had dismantled every flock of livestock, every crop, shelter, and tent they could find. The angel of the Lord was instructed to give Gideon a charge to destroy Baal. After Gideon destroyed the idol, the people were furious, saying, "We want whoever did this to be killed immediately." Gideon clearly needed a sign from God. He knew that what the angel had said was true, but he also needed confirmation.(Read: Judges 6)

Devotional Take Away

Anytime God wants to show up to heal, set free, restore, deliver, bless, help, and build, this is what God will do. We should let God show off sometimes. God feeds off of our praise for His showing off. He knows His power cannot be matched or placed in categories. God knows that his spiritual fish tank is greater than every ocean in the world. Let the power of God's presence fill your heart even now as you read these words. The best is yet to come, and God is not finished with you yet. He is clearly up to something, offering great opportunities as seen through the focal lenses of your dreams.

WATCH HOW THEY DRINK

God said to Gideon: "Everyone who laps with his tongue, the way
a dog laps, set on one side. And everyone who kneels to drink,
drinking with his face to the water, set to the other side."

JUDGES 7:5-6

Let's say you're having dinner at a restaurant, after a few bites into the meal you witness a blind date happening in real time, you might even see a married couple drinking a glass of wine on a date night. As you scan the other side of the area you notice young college students drinking and enjoying themselves at the bar. One student takes fireball shots, the other student drinks only draft beer. The shots get out of hand to the point security bouncer start directing the immature crowd out of the sports bar. The blind date you saw on the other side of the bar went sour to the point the lady started feeling uncomfortable leaving half of her drink the guy just bought for her.

Scripture Illustration

Gideon and his troops set up camp at Harod Springs near the hills of Moreh. The Midianites were camped north of Moreh waiting for war with the Israelites. Gideon had a total of 32,000 men. The wisdom of God kicked in, God said to Gideon "It will be too obvious that I give you the battle against the Midianites with the large number of men you have, the troops will think it was by there own power. There were still 22,000 troops that needed evaluation. God said "Take them to the water and watch how they drink. If they kneel drinking with there face to the water put them aside, if they lap the water like dogs set them on the other side.

This was a test God was showing Gideon between the difference of the "too good to fight" versus the "I'm desperate for a victory fight." Only three hundred men made the met the recruitment before stepping on the battlefield. The interesting part of this storyline is Gideon noticed a man who had a dream. The dream confirmed the battle begin winning. The man said. "I had this dream: A loaf of barley bread tumbled into the Midianite camp. It came to the tent and hit it so hard it collapsed. The tent fell!" His friend said, "This has to be the sword of Gideon son of Joash, the Israelite! God has turned Midian—the whole camp!—over to him." When God gives you the confirmation before the victory from a dream that just happened you know it's God.

Devotional Take Away

We might be living in selected friend zones that God might be pulling us away from. He might be saying I need you to cut some people off. Some people you hang out with might not be the ones fighting for you. They might just be against you faking that they can fight. Test "The way your friends drink." If there to good to pick you up when your car breaks down there kneeling down at the stream trying not to get wet. If they're the kind that plays like they don't remember who you are when you remind them of the money you let them borrow that's a knee bender.

If they enjoy your company, love to pray with you, study the Bible with you, go to church with you, take time to be connected with your family that means there in the 300. It means that they have a humble heart lapping the water with there tongues out of humility and sincerity. There might only be 300 left out of the 10,000 Instagram and Facebook friends that you really get to know on a deeper level. Take the time to study people in their various seasons to see if they can stick it out with you. Time is running out, we need real winners that aren't afraid of hard work, blood, sweat, and tears. Ask God to impart a new sense of discernment that outweighs the common battles of uncertainty. God has the power to give us clarity in clutter, joy in sorrow, passion for pain and destiny over devastation.

ABOUT THE AUTHOR

Dunamis Duplessis was born in Honolulu Hawaii July 23,1980. Nurtured in the environment of advanced theological teaching and biblical application bridged a greater zeal and dependency to serve God in ministry. Raised in the environment of teaching and preaching three times a week modeled a fresh trajectory and concept of leadership excellence. At the age of four he was enrolled into a Japanese American private school. There he mastered the curriculum of learning how to be fluent and efficient in Japanese. After graduating from high school overseas in 1998 he moved to San Antonio, Texas. A few months later he signed documents to be enlisted in the U.S Army as a infantryman in the 82nd Air borne division in Fort Bragg, NC. Years later he returned to Japan in 2009 to be a full-time English instructor in Yokohama, Japan.

On March 11th 2011 he witnessed and survived one of the most catastrophic earthquakes in Japanese history. The 9.1 earthquake deepen his love for God knowing that God spared his life for a higher calling. In 2014 he became a fishermen in Dutch Harbor, Alaska. He lived through a two day storm that almost took his life the second time. He knew there had to be deeper reasons for him living through two death wrenching experiences of testing. He vowed to God that he would give his life to Lord withholding nothing in appreciation for sparing his life twice. Dunamis currently resides in Plano, Texas married to the love of his life Khila Michelle Duplessis. His passion for christian writing has introduced a greater appreciation and desire for his assignment in ministry globally.